InstaWholesaler

Theresa Beneteau

i/Me
PUBLISHING GROUP
INSPIRE-MOTIVATE-EMPOWER

IME Publishing Group
1990 N California Blvd. Suite 20 PMB 1065
Walnut Creek, California 94596

1-866-726-6563
www.IMEPublishingGroup.com
Theresa Beneteau-1st ed.

Top 10 Questions You Should Ask About Wholesaling

https://app.bitly.com/Bo4pjwghIeQ/http://bit.ly/3yvMOxe

Table of Contents

Chapter 1

I am thrilled to share with you the simple steps to securing a wholesale deal and earning money. Getting paid is the most important part, so let's get started! Our first step will be to examine how your mind works—like a parachute, it only works when it's open. We will then cover topics such as the seller, due diligence, and Lights Camera Action.

A lot of money can be lost without due diligence. Preparing a winning offer, strategically setting up three viewings for contractors, communicating to your buyer's list that you are looking for a cash buyer is always super exciting. I love following my deals through to closing day. I have some value bonus strategies that I'm throwing in there as well.

How you present yourself to others will be key to doing good business. You want to appear as someone you wish to approach to do business with, negotiate with, meet for a coffee, give the keys to your house. You want to appear trustworthy and kind.

Again, it goes back to the parachute. Only when it's open, your mind is right. I can't stress this enough. If you're not thinking clearly, then you will not make quick informed decisions, nor will you attract motivated sellers. You will not attract motivated buyers. It is important to note; you will not attract the proper people if you do not have an open mind.

I would like you to answer these questions truthfully. What do you watch? Do you spend your time watching others make money or playing mindless computer games, sports, movies, or social media? Do you have Facebook, Instagram, or TikTok? Think about this question.

What do you listen to? Are you on YouTube? Are you listening to music? Are you just listening to other people talking? Are you engaging in gossip or filling your mind with news when people are talking negatively? What do you read? Some people read and then fall asleep. Are you reading news articles or gossip magazines.? Are you reading anything? Do you need to evolve? Are you reading self-help books or other books on real estate or are you watching YouTube videos? Do you like what you are reading? Be the keeper of your mind. As the gatekeeper of your brain, you have the power to filter out negativity from entering your mind.

Bad things are all around us. We just went through the pandemic, so it's important to take care of our mental health. What are we putting into our minds? Could you take advice from broke friends, people with zero real estate investing experience, and people who are just satisfied with their financial situation? They are quite content being at their nine-to-five. What is it you know? Who are you talking to? Relatives can be great, but they might also be the people who discourage you and tell you not to do certain things.

Be mindful of who you are talking to and seek advice from people who are where you are going. Have you ever taken advice from successful people like Warren Buffett, Jim Rohn, Tony Robbins, Darren Hardy, or Robert Kiyosaki (also known as the Rich Dad or Poor Dad)? It's important to be mindful of who you allow to influence your decisions.

The people you listen to can impact your life, so choose wisely. Please take a moment to reflect on the following text: Write down these things. It's important to know what you're doing now and where you stand. Take inventory of your thoughts and the things that fuel your desires, goals, and dreams. What is on your mind that motivates you?

When you're considering vacation, housing, or family support, where do you want to be? How are you planning to support your family? What actions are you taking to enhance your knowledge and skills so that you can achieve your goals? Are you merely daydreaming about your aspirations without setting a timeline for their accomplishment, thinking that they might not come true for you? What efforts are you making towards your goals? During the day, what are some things that make you wonder if they are possible? What are you reading? What are you watching? What are you listening to?

It's important to expand your mind so your desires, goals, and dreams can come true. Take a deep dive into these activities and make a personal inventory of everything you're doing now. This will help you understand what you're currently doing and where you need to focus your efforts. It's important to take this step if you want to achieve your goals.

What do you do to inspire creative thinking outside of your daily work routine? Are you only looking forward to the middle of the week and the weekend for relaxation, or are you constantly exploring investment opportunities? Are you considering starting a side hustle to eventually replace your day job? What is it you're focusing on that will compel you to achieve more? A big part of it is knowing what will motivate you in the future.

Consider the people you spend most of your time with, as your net worth is the average of the six people you associate with the most. Think about your six closest friends and ask yourself if they are better off financially than you are. Are they more comfortable? Or perhaps they are where you want to be someday. Or are you the smartest one in your group? I don't mean this from an egoistic perspective. The biggest thing is, if you're the smartest person in your group, you should be capable of adding people to that group and changing it for the better. I'm not suggesting that you get rid of everyone. That's not what I'm promoting. I encourage you to surround yourself with people who are already where you want to be. Often, we settle for the company of those who are not at the same level as us, but this doesn't help us grow or reach our goals. Instead, we should aim to be with individuals who inspire us to be our best and challenge us to step out of our comfort zone. This way, we can achieve what we truly aspire to be.

What do you typically do in a day? Do you sleep, work, play, go to the gym, or party? Or do you have no time for any of these activities? How do you divide your time, especially when you're driving or have no extra time? Are you listening to the radio or are you listening to self-help Kindle ebooks or YouTube videos? What are you doing that is going to help you? I understand we need to sleep, work and have leisure time. But the most important thing is to take stock, to take inventory. If you own a business, you will need to figure out your opening hours, what you will do during those hours, when you will restock the shelves, and when you need to take an inventory of everything in there.

We need to ensure that we balance the till and cash out whatever is left. When you take a closer look at how you spend your time throughout the day, you'll realize that everyone, successful or not, has the same 24 hours. The difference lies in being mindful of how you use that time, because once it's gone, it can't be reclaimed.

Although money can be earned, time is a non-renewable resource. One of the biggest considerations is how you spend your time within the 24 hours of a day. Even Warren Buffett has the same amount of time, so it's important to think about how you can use it to your advantage. Will you use that time to improve yourself or simply waste it? Are these really our only choices? The thing is, I already agree with you even before you mentioned it. Some people just don't realize that there are other options available. They don't even consider that there are choices to be made. All I am suggesting is that there are options. Once you realize this, you realize certain activities are mindless and won't help you make money or learn anything new. For instance, while going to the gym will help your body, think about what you do on your way there and back. Are you maximizing your 24 hours?

Where do you want to live? A lot of us don't describe where we want to live in detail. We just want to live in a house. I want a big house. I want my own bathroom. I want a pool. I want to be on the water. The biggest thing we often neglect is visualizing our goals. We should take the time to close our eyes and envision what we truly want, such as three bedrooms on the main floor and two bedrooms upstairs. I suggest to many people that they should visit the property they are interested in, call a real estate agent, attend an open house, and explore the options. Dreaming is great, but it is pointless if you don't have any plans to turn those dreams into reality. If you're interested in buying a house, it's important to focus on what you truly want. Whether it's a specific neighborhood, city, state, or country, be as detailed as possible. Envision your future home and imagine the backyard, the waterfront, the garage, or anything that matters to you. Your motivation could be to provide for your family, to prepare for future children, or to live in an area with wonderful schools or for retirement. Whatever your reasons, take ownership of your dream house and keep it in mind. The possibilities in real estate are endless.

If you can dream it, you can make it happen, because if you weren't given the dream, then you weren't given the ability to make it happen. If you can dream it, you can become it. Let that resonate with you. If you're really honing in on those possibilities, whether on your own or online, take a closer look at them.

It's like a GPS. If you get in a car and you don't program your GPS, it will not give you any directions. It will not say make a left, make a right, go here, go there. It will not say anything, because there is nothing to tell you since you haven't programmed it. This is part of the program. What type of car do you want to drive? Do you know the color of the interior? Do you know the features? How fast of a car do you want? Do you want a Lambo? Do you want a Ferrari? Do you want a Corvette? I have a Corvette, and I love it. Do you know what you want? Some people may prefer a less flashy car, and that's okay. Perhaps you're happy with your current vehicle but want something newer. If you already have a new car, that's great! However, if you're considering purchasing a backup car or buying someone else a car, that's also worth considering.

It's about looking at a situation and asking yourself how you can use it to bless someone else. If the situation is about you, own it and start believing in the possibility of your dreams. Many of us don't pursue our dreams because we don't think they'll come true, and we don't want to be deceived. That's a big part of why we don't do it. Real estate is not a get-rich-quick scheme. If you're looking for a quick way to make money, then I'm not the right person to listen to. I suggest you stop right now and don't waste your time with me and just call it a day. If you will put in the effort and lay the foundation for your work, I can guarantee you will achieve success in due time. So, roll up your sleeves and get to work!

It's better to get rich slowly than never get rich at all. Am I going to teach you the fundamentals? Yes. Am I going to teach you how to do this? Yes. Is it going to happen overnight, rain money? That's not how it happens. That would be illegal. Keep that in mind as well. We want you to go out there and be able to make a living and create wealth, generate wealth and have something that you can be proud of.

Who will you help when you become financially free? Are you looking at saving up money for a family? Are you considering retirement for your parents, spouse, or yourself? Perhaps you're considering giving more to your church, local shelters, or food banks. It's important to remember that giving should not stem from a selfish desire to accumulate wealth, but from a place of generosity and compassion. It's important to think about how we can help and positively impact others. There are many opportunities to do so, such as providing affordable housing or assisting in the care of elderly individuals who are often understaffed due to a lack of funding. It's important to ask ourselves, *who can we help and how can we contribute?* Write down your thoughts and ideas.

Wouldn't it be nice one day if you overhear someone saying, "Oh, you know what? I don't have the money for rent this month." How would you feel if suddenly you said, "Hey, you know what, I got it and here's a couple extra months." How would that make you feel inside if you could help someone, whether it's family, a friend, a stranger?

Imagine standing in a grocery store line and seeing a mother in front of you struggling to afford food and diapers for her baby. How would it feel to offer your help and say, "Hey, I can help you with that?" We can give others many blessings as we become successful, including sharing the knowledge we gain with others. This is what paying it forward is all about-it's not just about us, but also about helping others. Real estate is simply a vehicle to get us to where we want to go, and the biggest thing is knowing where is it you want to go and being very clear on that.

What kind of experience would you like to create for yourself or others? Do you have children or know any? Are you a big kid? Do you have a sense of adventure and want to create some new experiences? Do you want to travel? Do you want to explore? I love wildlife. That's my thing. Do you want to go to a jungle, to Africa, to Arizona and see the Grand Canyon, or visit Canada? Is there somewhere in the world that you want to visit? Do you want to go to Italy? Would you like to experience scuba diving, fishing, swimming in an ocean, or swimming with dolphins? There are so many experiences. What would it be like if you suddenly said to a couple of your friends, why don't we go on this trip?

Don't worry, I'm picking up the tab? What would that look like if you did that with your family, siblings, parents, grandparents, significant other? Writing down what you want to experience can help you get excited about it. What do you want to create? I want you to aim big on this because a regular nine-to-five job doesn't always allow you to do what you want. Your boss determines when you can take time off, how long you can be away, and even when you can go to the washroom. They also tell you how many sick days or bereavement days you can take.

They're not encouraging you every day to what you want. What experiences do you want to create? What would the experience be if you didn't have to work at your job? Now, don't get me wrong, if you love your job, I'm not saying you have to quit your job, you can stay at your job. All I'm saying is that if you didn't need the money, think about that. If you didn't need the money, would you do something different Monday morning? Would you still go to the regular job that you have now if money was not a reason you went there?

Some individuals are incredibly passionate about their work and do not intend to quit. That is great. Real estate can be a nice little side hustle. Being able to provide people with more than they need is a blessing. Again, write this down, just let it all pour out, let whatever come into your mind. Open up that mind, like that parachute that we talked about in the beginning. Just open up your mind. Let it just really expand. Why do you want these things? Why are these things important to you? There are lots of details. You might say that you want to work at a particular job and pursue something on the side. Well, I want a winter car and a summer car. Why not both? So why am I writing this down? I know the answer. For me, my journey in real estate began at 21. I just knew that I was meant for more. I knew that there's something out there and I really had a burning desire to work for myself and not for someone else. I don't want someone to decide how long I can take my break, how many vacation days I can have. I wanted a lot of freedom.

I realized that having a job would limit my freedom. I want to do what I want, when I want, where I want, and with whom I want, for as long as I want. Bosses really frown on being able to do that. Having this freedom was important to me. When I was growing up, my parents neglected me because they had to work. They had to work different shifts. Mom was on days and Dad was on afternoons just so I did not have to be with a babysitter and so I could see them. I saw the strain on them because they couldn't even be together at the same time. My thoughts were, *When I get married, I don't want that for myself. I want something better. When I have a child, I want to make sure that I am present for them. I want to stay at home and attend to my child's needs whenever required.*

I broke my arm when I was 12 years old and my dad couldn't be there because he was at work, he couldn't come home. That was hard. Because of growing up like this, I didn't want this to happen in my adult life. I wanted to purchase my home, and I didn't want to rent. I wanted to move out on my own.

I recall a memory where there was a newspaper article about a builder who was selling a property. I asked my boss for an hour off to see it, and he got upset. I went to see the property and witnessed the sale between the builder and another man. They shook hands, and the deal was done. I felt disappointed and frustrated that I had missed out on the opportunity. However, I was determined to find my chance, so I kept looking. Eventually, I went to my parents and told them I wanted to buy a house. They loaned me the money for the down payment, and I bought my first house.

I then realized, after buying my first house, I might become poor as all my money would be invested in the house. This made me question if buying the house was a good idea in the first place, despite it being what I wanted. A friend of mine came over and suggested that she would be interested in renting my house. I was surprised to hear this and asked her how much she would pay. She offered a higher amount than what I was paying for the property. This gave me an idea, and I immediately agreed to the deal. I realized I could make money in real estate! Being I had no money, my first approach was wholesaling.

Back then, they didn't have a name for that yet. LOL I was involved in wholesaling, I would put offers on properties and then sell the contracts to someone else. They would close the deal, and I would make a profit. Wholesaling opened up an entire world of opportunities for me, even though I faced challenges like recessions, job losses, bankruptcy and having to get a job again. Despite these setbacks, I continued to come up with new ways to succeed in the business.

Despite facing many obstacles, like losing my job, bankruptcy, and high interest rates, I was still figuring things out on my own with no guidance or coach. I was relying on some people, and they were trying to figure it out. We would fail together.

It was my *why* that kept pushing me forward. I knew I wanted more out of life, and I was determined to figure out how to make it happen. I kept asking myself, "What do I need to do?" The answer always came back to my *why*-my reason for wanting more. I knew that if I stayed focused on that, I would make my dreams a reality. This is the reason I can't stress the why enough. The why is the juice, the why is the reason you want this, and I've been able to leverage my why.

I've been able to stay away from having to get a job the last 20-plus years. I remember taking a psychology course where I recalled my parents had worked in a factory. I also worked in a factory for one shift, but I hated it and decided never to go back. However, my parents instilled in me a strong work ethic, teaching me to wake up early and work hard. These skills have been useful to me in pursuing my own goals rather than just making money for someone else. Without a plan, you will end up fitting into someone else's plan.

That was the one thing I didn't want; I didn't want to fit into someone else's plan. I didn't want to make somebody else rich on my labor or on my work ethic. I didn't want to be the one to show up early and work late. That was who I was, and I knew very early on that I was going to be taken advantage of as an employee because they could, so I just knew that I didn't want to trade my time for money.

Those were some things that ironically enough hit me. My current husband worked in a factory, and I was able to retire him using real estate because I didn't like him even being in a factory. My husband was working in a factory, and we were still limited on when we could take time off because his boss would decide our schedule. I didn't like this lack of control, so my motivation to change the situation was very strong. I knew I wanted to buy a property where I could take care of my parents, and I could achieve that goal.

When I look at all the things that I wanted, these were all the reasons that these things were very important to me. Family means everything to me. The driving force behind this was the desire to give back to my family. I am so grateful I have been able to do that and to even grow beyond that. That was my entire mission. I think initially, the idea of being self-employed was driven by a desire to not work for somebody else, to not have a boss. It was all about my own wants and needs. Over time, however, this changed. I thought more about how I could use my skills to help others. I realized I can have both-a successful business and a fulfilling way to help others. Achieving this will take time, effort, dedication, and some late nights. It won't be as easy as watching a video and suddenly having money raining down on you. However, I can tell you that the strength of your motivation is crucial. If your reasons for pursuing this path don't make you emotional, they're not strong enough. Without a strong why, you'll give up as soon as things get tough. So, make sure you write down all the details and keep them close.

What emotions or feelings will you have when you achieve these things? When I sat down and made a list of things I wanted, it made me think about the emotions I would feel if they happened. Looking at my list, I realized that if everything on it came true, my life would look very different. I thought about how my daily routine would change and how I would spend my time if I wasn't bored.

It's really important to allow yourself to expand emotionally and fully experience your feelings. Take a few minutes to look over your list of desires-the house, car, job, and side hustle you want. Allow yourself to really visualize having those things, even if it means leaving your current job. I want to care for my family, whatever that looks like, and I want to bless other people. How would it feel? How do you think you would feel? Would you feel fulfilled? Success, without fulfillment, is the ultimate failure.

If you get to the end of this and you get everything you want, you go okay; I did it. There's an emptiness. Robin Williams is a great example. Everything that he set out to do, he did, and in the end, he took his own life because he felt unfulfilled. We should be truly grateful for what we have. After we experience true fulfillment, we feel motivated to continue pursuing it because of the emotions and satisfaction it provides.

I really want to invite you to be in touch with yourself. Let your emotions stir and share stories with loved ones. As you go on your journey and start earning money, think about what memories you can create for the people you are taking with you in your car. For instance, going to the park and spending quality time with them. You're able to afford first-class tickets and a plane. What would that be like for your family and friends? What would it be like if you hired a cleaner for your parents or for yourself in your own place? What would it be like to pay for a private jet and bring 20 people that you know, and go across the world for tea?

Go somewhere extravagant for an afternoon. It's important to create memories because once time has passed, it's gone forever. Yesterday is gone and cannot be returned. What experiences could you share and create for others, that suddenly, in 5-10, 50-100 years from now that someone else is going to remember? You could even be near foster families or orphanages. What experiences could you bring to those children? These are just some examples.

What would it be like if a lot of people were sitting around, and they were talking about how generous you were, and how you made an event happen? At a hospital, a woman was giving birth while her mother, who had cancer, was being treated at another hospital in a different city. The woman expressed her sadness to the nurse that her mother could not see her grandchild being born. However, the hospital staff took a compassionate step and arranged for the grandmother to be flown in to witness the birth of her granddaughter. When looking at such opportunities, it's important to have someone in charge to facilitate them, as exemplified by the hospital's case.

If someone is solely focused on their job and their own interests, they may only be concerned about the bottom line. For example, when a woman gives birth in a hospital, it could be just a matter of paying a certain amount and then leaving with no additional support or care. However, if there is. someone with a bigger perspective, they may be concerned with creating a memorable experience for the mother and making it a lifelong memory. The presence of her mother during childbirth is a precious moment that cannot be recreated, and it is essential to create such memories. These are just a few examples of how one can be generous, such as through donations. Some people prefer to remain anonymous when doing good deeds, which is perfectly fine.

Onto another example. Many people are discussing the kindness of a stranger paying for education. There are some gifted children who cannot afford an education. This could negatively impact their future.

If you spread your knowledge and skills to your kids, parents, or friends, who may not be as fortunate as you, you can make a real difference. You can learn something new and use it to help others. Harness that and own it. I look at this like it's my responsibility that they have wonderful memories and good stories. It's my responsibility to help people around me who are struggling, especially if there's something that I can do about it. Don't get me wrong, I'm not into giving a handout, I'm more into giving a hand-up. You have the power to put a smile on someone's face and change their story. You can create a memory that they will cherish for the rest of their life and show them that humanity is more than what the news portrays it to be.

There are many ways to impact someone on different levels. What are your dreams and desires? Dig deep and aim high. What if these things happen? How would you feel? For example, that guy over there looks like he's just flailing in the wind. He's doing some kind of dance, but it seems like he's putting in a lot of effort. It's like when you're really pushing yourself to your limits - anything is possible.

Sometimes, we just need to look at a situation and believe that anything is possible. However, when we start something new or feel excited, we can also experience fear. This feeling is often referred to as *imposter syndrome*, when we doubt our own abilities and feel like we don't really know what we're doing. I'm shy. It's all about dreaming big, digging deep, and acting like you can't fail. There's a saying, *love like you've never been hurt.* I don't remember the rest of it, but it's a big part of it. What if you made money in real estate no matter what you did? What if success was inevitable regardless of what you said?

I'm not a motivational coach. I will not sit here and motivate you. Motivation is like a shower. If you take one today, you're going to need one tomorrow. It's the rocket fuel that power the dreams and desires. Why are you doing this? Do you know what you want? The bigger you go, the more success you're going to have. The bigger your goal, the more you will accomplish. For instance, if you aim to make $100 in real estate, you will achieve just that.

Instead, you want to make $10 million in real estate. This can absolutely 100% happen if you dream it and create it. You work to get it and don't stop till you do. I had a saying a while back: *This is my mountain, and I'm going to climb it. If I don't make it to the top, I'll die trying right next to it.* This was my mantra, and it served me well. My motivation was unwavering, and it kept me an active investor for over 35 years.

This is all I do full time, but my dreams have long surpassed me. It's about putting a smile on other people's faces. How do you get what you want? Your life will become unrecognizable as you expand, as you dream, as you own it and say, I'm going to make this happen. Suddenly, you're going to say, wow, I didn't think that was going to happen. You see that when you made a phone call, that person called you back. I have had some of my students report back to me saying that people are treating them differently. One of my students even told me that someone asked why they were smiling all the time.

It is how you show up. When suddenly you do these things and you show up differently, the surrounding results change, people change. If you're walking around with your smile on, people are going to wonder what you're up to. It's just going to cause conversation. When someone doesn't have a smile, give them one of yours.

We will talk about your state of mind. Your state of mind is how do you show up? Are you groomed? Are you well dressed? Is your head up high? Do you look other people in the eye? Do you have good posture? Are you well spoken? Do you have a positive attitude? Do you like what you look like?

I would be scared to see a boxer show up in a negative state in a boxing ring. He's showing up prepared. He's ready. He's like, let's go. How do you present yourself? You have a scheduled call or you're planning to meet someone in person for business, such as a seller, buyer, real estate agent, lawyer, or lender. It's important to consider how you're presenting yourself. How are you preparing to make a positive and professional impression? Are you showing up with confidence or are you going to hide? How could you approach the situation with a positive attitude? One of my coaches suggested that when you're feeling scared, place your hands on your hips and stand still for a couple of minutes before approaching someone to talk. Would you consider trying that?

When you feel confident, you carry yourself differently. Your shoulders go back, and you exude a certain energy. People can sense this confidence, just as they can sense fear. People say dogs can smell fear. People can smell fear too. If you show up hesitant, you look untrustworthy. If you show up with confidence and friendliness, you are in a good state. I wanted to share a helpful tip. Have you ever tried looking at yourself in the mirror for two minutes straight? It can be challenging at first, but it's a great way to improve your focus and confidence. Maintain eye contact with yourself the whole time. You might get distracted or look away, but just keep refocusing on your eyes. Doing this every day can really help boost your self-awareness and self-esteem. It's common to laugh when we feel uncomfortable, but we need to get used to being uncomfortable. I will tell you, there is no money in your comfort zone. Your dreams will not happen in your comfort zone.

How do I know this? Well, if the opposite were true, you would have already acquired everything you desire. You wouldn't be listening to my words right now. Therefore, it's clear that you need to push yourself out of your comfort zone further than you ever have. Personally, I haven't been in my comfort zone for a long time. I haven't even visited it in a while. Whenever I feel comfortable, I know I must be doing something wrong. If there is something that I don't feel like doing, I know I must do it.

When you show up with a positive attitude and a plan, you increase the likelihood of a positive outcome. I know I want to buy that property. I'm going in there, I'm putting in an offer, we're going to sit down, we're going to negotiate and we're going to figure it out. Walking into a meeting with confidence is much better than hoping for a good outcome.

I cannot stress enough that your state is everything. You get one chance to meet people, and you want to make a good first impression. The way you present yourself during your first meeting with someone is crucial, as it shapes their perception of you. I'm not implying that you need to wear a fancy suit or an evening gown, but it's important to at least dress appropriately and presentably, for instance, wearing a clean collared shirt or jacket. Even if you cannot afford expensive clothing, you can still find good options at resale or consignment stores. If you have the money to spare, invest in a jacket and a few shirts that fit your budget.

All I'm saying is step it up, be groomed, also make sure that your hair is done nicely. When I was younger, I didn't want to have to dress up; I didn't want to do my hair; I didn't want to have to put makeup on. I didn't want to have to do any of that. What I realize is that this is how I see myself- I'm a tomboy who loves fishing and everything outdoors. I still enjoy dirt bike riding, motorcycle riding, four-wheeling and all that stuff. For me, comfort comes in a baseball cap, a t-shirt, and sweats.

I realized I was losing credibility when I was showing up like that. I was losing credibility because of how I looked. I was being judged for that, not because I wasn't knowledgeable or because I did not know what I was doing. We can sit here, and we can say we don't judge others. In reality, we make a judgement in 10 seconds. Within 10 seconds, we know if we're going to like the person and the first thing that we see is how they look. If you're showing up at a business meeting, your appearance matters a lot.

When you're in a good state, your internal dialogue, or story should include positive affirmations such as "I am good enough, I come from abundance, I am smart enough, I am attractive enough, I am capable, I will succeed, and I can do this." When you have this positive mindset, you will feel more motivated and confident. Your positive story will help you achieve your goals.

I have noticed that when I hear positive things in my mind, it motivates me to take action, and I feel encouraged to do better. It's like I can hear people cheering me on, saying, "You can do it! Come on!" Your mindset can affect your actions and the story you create for yourself. That's why it's crucial to prioritize your state of mind before anything else. Once you put yourself in a positive state, everything else will fall into place and you'll see a significant change in your outlook and actions.

Sometimes we come from different places in our lives, and we hear different voices in our heads. Some people say that hearing voices in your head is a sign of craziness, but I disagree. We all hear voices in our heads, don't we? The voice that made me doubt my sanity because I heard voices did not differ from the voice that makes you doubt your own. You have a voice too, right?

We all have the voices in our head, we all have an internal dialogue. These are the things that you're going to be fighting all the way through this journey. I have encountered many students who claim to be positive, motivated, and have undergone personal development. However, as soon as I give them a challenge, their negative story takes over and they lose their positive state. This happens because they get out of their positive state and fail to remain motivated.

I was at a coaching session one night and I looked at my student, and I said, "Okay, are you ready for a challenge?" He said, "Well, it depends on what it is."

I told him he should put an offer on a property this week. He responded by saying that he plans to put two offers in instead. It's all about being in the right mindset and feeling like you can make things happen. This is really important.

Regarding strategy, it's important to feel confident and in control. When approaching a task, it's helpful to have a mindset of being capable and prepared. Even if challenges arise, it's best to believe in yourself and trust in your abilities to overcome them. When you're in a positive state of mind and have a positive story in your head, it becomes easier to find solutions to your problems. Your mindset becomes resourceful, and you ask powerful questions. You feel confident, positive, and ready to take on challenges. You can stand tall with your hands on your hips and say to yourself, "I can do this."

Suddenly, I wonder how I can make this happen.

Some questions that you may ask yourself when considering real estate investment include: Who can help me solve this problem? Has anyone done this before? Who has the financial resources to invest in real estate? Where can I find motivated sellers and cash buyers? How can I raise capital? What steps can I take to market myself?"

Your mind will expand when you hear these questions because the mind unlocks options, and opportunities show up. One of my mentors once said that becoming a millionaire isn't just about the money, but also about the person you need to become to achieve it. When I was on my way to my first million, I remember looking at the goal and feeling overwhelmed. I wondered if I could do it, as it seemed like it would take forever to reach that amount. It was a lot of money to aim for, and I wasn't sure if I could achieve it.

As I was navigating this, I remembered when I heard Jim Rohn say that it wasn't about getting to the million dollars, but it was about the journey that I had to go on. I had to put myself in a positive state to shape my story positively. From there, I could develop a strategy and ask myself, "What do I need to do?" Now, I can listen to others and be guided to where I want to go.

It's very important to listen to people, to be engaged and absorb what they have to say. It is good to have an open dialogue. To have a million dollars, you don't just make it, you attract it. The money already exists in the world. It's just a matter of drawing it towards you. Money is simply an energy that you must attract towards yourself.

Many of us are constantly chasing financial freedom, but do we really understand what it takes to achieve it? To reach this goal, we must become someone who is patient, diligent, focused, and able to stay the course. We must also learn how to stay in a peak state so that we can access the inner motivation necessary to succeed.

I'm a big fan of Tony Robbins and his emphasis on peak state. Every morning, he starts off, doing a cold plunge in 50- or 56-degree water. I've done it three times, but each time everything changed. When you're in colder water, you can't think of anything else.

This is an example of having the confidence to do something new and stretch your mind to know you can jump into a cold plunge. Who do you have to become to do this? If you won't jump in the cold plunge, then you can talk yourself out of anything. I am a strong believer in the philosophy of 'If I can't do that, then I must do that.' I remember my first visit to a day spa where I was advised to take a cold plunge at least three times during my visit for the sake of my health. I considered it non-negotiable and followed their advice without hesitation.

If I am in a focused and prepared state, I will listen carefully to the instructions given to me and will follow them without hesitation. However, if I am not in the right state of mind, my negative thoughts and emotions may take over, making me reluctant to follow through with the task at hand. For instance, if the task involves jumping into cold water, my negative thoughts may convince me it is too unpleasant to do. In such cases, I need to snap out of my negative frame of mind and focus on finding a solution to complete the task without having to face the unpleasant situation directly.

One needs to get out of one's comfort zone to grow. I walked on fire in November 2018 in New Jersey. It was during one of the *Unleash the Power Within* events with Tony Robbins. Walking on 2000 degrees of fire was an intense experience, but I highly recommend you try it. This was a total game changer. I did this to open my mind and get my state of mind right.

I believed I had to have the right state of mind to get through this and get out of my comfort zone. I had to prove to myself that I could walk over 2000-degree coals and reach the other side. After the accomplishment of reaching the other side, I became so emotional because of the freedom I felt from this accomplishment. My feet did not have one blister on them either. This represented a symbolic moment for me, telling me I can accomplish anything.

I was going through hard moments in my life. I also hadn't really made the commitment that real estate was going to make me feel better. I was struggling because I was trying to make money. I was trying this endeavor out, and it was a slow process. It was painful and long and the interest rates were not good. I then got a coach, and that was a game changer. Having a coach made the difference. The coach helped me reach the other side and gave me guidance to get me to where I wanted to be.

There are only two motivators: pain and pleasure. When you get to the breaking point, you know this must stop. One breaking point was regarding my weight. I decided I had enough. I could then lose a substantial amount of weight, which increased my health dramatically.

I knew that cancer ran in my family, and I became mindful of what I ate and what I put into my body. The pain motivated me. I did not want cancer, and the stress of this possibility caused pain for me and that led me to change. It goes back to what I talked about before, regarding my parents working all the time. I did not want that either, and I had to change this for my future.

Then there's pleasure, the reward. My rewards were: I don't have to work at my job anymore. I can help my husband retire and take care of my elderly parents. I could also be home with my son. I struggled a lot during my early childhood. I learned that pain and pleasure were the two things that motivated me. You learn if the pain is bad enough, you will change.

There's a story about a man who walked by a porch where a dog was howling in pain. The man walked up to the porch and went into the store and came out. The next day, the man did the same thing, and the dog was still there, whining in pain. This happened again the third day, and the dog was now crying. The man realized that if something hurts enough, we will change.

That man walked into the store, and he asked the owner why the dog was crying, and the owner explained the dog was sitting on a nail. The man then asked why the dog wasn't moving, and the owner replied that the pain wasn't enough to make him move. The man wondered if the same thing applies to humans. The man realized that if something hurts enough, we will change. Does the pain have to be unbearable for us to act? If we are comfortable, we may not take any action, but if we are uncomfortable enough, we will do anything to make the situation better.

There will be days when you won't feel like working in real estate anymore. You'll reach a point where you don't want to make another phone call, and people might get angry with you. Some might even call you a scammer or a con artist. You'll lose friends and family, and the journey won't be easy. It's not a golden road that lies ahead of you, and I won't lie to you. But if you're not feeling enough pain, then you won't get off the nail. And if you don't get off the nail, you'll be content to stay put, even if it hurts. Some of us are so used to the pain that we don't want to move, and we keep talking about the pain to everyone.

Some people will only complain about the nails. It's like self-pity, like a self-fulfilling prophecy. We want people to know that we're in pain and want to stay there. We don't want to get off the nail. We don't want to change. When the pain becomes unbearable, is it worth enduring? I know one person who was totally comfortable. He had a successful paying job, and everything was great. Suddenly, something went wrong at his job, and he called me up and told me something went wrong at his job. He told me he didn't want to go back. He wanted to try real estate and make it work for him. I told him I wanted to make this happen for him.

The moral of the story is, until all his pain was deep enough, he would not get off the nail. He would not make a move because he was comfortable. Sadly enough, some of us can just be comfortable getting by. We can just be okay with that regular paycheck every two weeks, whatever salary, whether it's $50,000 a year or $500,000 a year, we get comfortable. We are satisfied with its close enough, it's good enough. If it hurts bad enough, I assure you, you will change.

But until it hurts bad enough, you will not have the motivation, and it will not push you and propel you to do what you need to do to get to have success. Think of something that you know has caused you pain in the past. For example, it could be being overweight, broke, unemployed, living with lazy roommates or your parents, not having enough money for food, or as a child, not having a car. Take a moment to reflect on this.

Perhaps this scenario has occurred multiple times in your life, even repeatedly. At some point, you decided you had enough. You resolved not to continue the same pattern, behavior, or substance abuse any longer. The pain you experienced was intense enough to prompt you to make a change. Suddenly, you realized you could no longer tolerate your current situation. You could no longer endure your current job, your financial struggles, or your living conditions. The state of the economy, rising interest rates, and people losing their homes only added to your distress.

You know when you reach a point where you've had enough, you wonder, "What do I need to do? Just tell me and I'll do it." You need to feel that something is propelling you forward. There are only two fuels for this: pain and pleasure. I want you to contemplate about what motivates you. Is it because you now have a job after struggling to find one? Or you've realized that you want to go to college or university after finishing high school.

What motivated you to gain more education? Why did you choose your job? What made you select your car or the place where you live? Why did you decide to stay at home or move out? Whatever your choices are, they were driven by some motivation within you. Even the smallest decisions, like taking a shower in the morning, might be motivated by the discomfort of unpleasant body odor. It's important to understand what causes this discomfort and pain, and how you can address it to achieve your goals. Instead of me telling you what to do, the key is to find what works for you. Perhaps being single is the right choice for you.

You might say, I'm tired of being single. Enough is enough. I'm going out and asking someone out on a date. I've got to make a change. Whatever made you decide, you just said, enough is enough. I can't stay here anymore. This situation isn't comfortable. I'm tired of it. That's it. It's done. So, think about that moment. Remember what made you say, "Aha!" because we all have it. There's always something that drives us.

I really want you to delve deep into that and think of something that brought you pleasure. For example, asking someone on a date and they said yes. You bought a new car or a new to you car. You aced an interview, and you got the job. You fit in your pants again, because you'd gained so much weight now you lost it. You went to the gym. Sometimes we feel good just going into the parking lot. This time you went inside, you did your benching, the sit-ups, and the curls; you did all that. You worked up a sweat, and you got out to your car, and you went *yeah, nailed it*. After completing the task, did you feel satisfied knowing that it brought you pleasure? You did what you needed to do to achieve your desires.

The pain pushes us, and the pleasure pulls us. Let's take a moment to reflect on what makes us feel good. Think about experiences that brought you pleasure and made you feel good. Sometimes, we need to step out of our comfort zone to discover new things that bring us joy. I encourage you to write down a specific time when you felt pleasure from doing something that required you to step out of your comfort zone. If you can recall an experience that brought you pleasure, then you know what works for you. Remember, pulling from pleasure can help you in finding joy in your life.

If something hurt you in the past and you changed it, you know that pain works for you. What you're really doing is proving what I'm saying is right, and it works for you. It doesn't matter who you are or where you are in the world, there are two forces that can help you achieve what you want. I don't like using the word 'motivation' because what really matters is understanding these two forces. These forces are going to push you forward and pull you towards your goal. The power of knowing why you want to achieve something is key.

For instance, let's say there is a two-story building on fire, and I ask you to walk across a two by four placed between that building and another. This would mean walking two stories up in the air. Would you do it? Of course not.

Imagine this scenario: You are in a building that is on fire, and you need to get to another building where someone you love is located. The only way to get there is by walking on a thin two by four plank. If you don't make it, the person you love will perish. Will you take the risk and walk on that plank? The answer is yes, because your motivation has changed. The buildings are still on fire; the plank is still thin, but your reason for crossing has changed. By the way, the plank is not actually two inches by four inches, it's just called a two by four plank. It's one and a half inches by three and a half inches.

Suddenly, your reason for doing something changed. When the reason behind something changes, and you ask *why* it must happen, you become more determined and focused. Regardless of the obstacles in your way, you are determined to figure things out and achieve your goal. For instance, you may need to enter a building, and the entrance may be high off the ground or very narrow. However, when you have a strong why, you will take on any challenge to reach your objective.

This is the burning desire that you need to have within your belly. You really need to look at it and go, okay, why do I want it? Some people would say, well, it's for the money. All right, I get that, but what is that money going to do? Money is just paper; you can burn it. I mean, it's not legal to burn it, but you can. What can you do with the money? You can use the money for experiences, trips, helping other people. When you look, why are you doing it? Those are the compelling moments. Look at that car and who's driving it. They are laser-focused, pausing on the wheel, not even blinking. The same thought goes into entering the burning building, I must do it. It's non-negotiable.

It's important to put yourself in a confident state of mind when pursuing your goals. Hoping for success is not enough. You need to have a coherent plan of action and believe in your ability to make it work. I often remind my students that hope is not a strategy. Instead of saying, "I hope my offer gets accepted" or "I hope things will change," it's better to check your mindset and say, "This is how I'm going to do it" and "This is why it's going to work."

If your state of mind is feeling anxious and lacking confidence, please remember action conquers fear. It's not just about sitting there and meditating like Patrick is doing. My son loved the show called *SpongeBob* and I remember all the times we watched tons of episodes of SpongeBob together. We would relate to SpongeBob, and everything had to do with it. But when you look at Patrick in that picture, you realize it's not just about meditation. It's about hoping that a seller will call you, that a cash buyer will show up, that a realtor will find you, throughout the power of hope and positivity.

All I'm saying is that you can't just expect things to happen. You're going to have to go make it happen. The great thing is that my program is put together for a person who's never done a wholesale deal and who's never done any kind of real estate before. We can take the entire strategy out of the equation. We can show you exactly what to do. It's important to get in the right mindset and not give up easily.

If you passively watch something taking no action, then you cannot expect any change to happen. However, if you are fully invested in my program and follow my instructions diligently by taking notes, using the pause button, and repeating and rewinding as needed, then you are truly implementing what you have learned and will see actual results. Here, you won't need to rely on hope to achieve your goals.

"Focus on the turn, not the wall" is expert advice from a race car driver that can apply to many aspects of life. For instance, a racecar driver who focuses on the wall will inevitably crash into it. However, if they focus on making the turn, they will eventually correct their spin and make it through.

Whenever we face something new or unfamiliar, there's a learning curve that can cause us to spin out of control. We can either choose to give up and crash or focus on our goals and get out of the spin, staying the course. Think of a challenging experience you have overcome in the past. What strategies did you use to make it happen? We've all gone through tough situations that have led us to make changes in our lives. If you're here, it's not a coincidence. There's a reason you've landed here at this time in your life and are reading my book. It is not divine intervention, but an intentional decision on your part.

When students come to me, they're often in the middle of a tailspin, thinking that everything needs to happen now. However, I encourage them to focus on where they want to go. What's their why? Where are they headed? Instead of staring at the wall, let's focus on the turn and look to the left. That's the biggest thing that a lot of us do, focus on the wall. We crash and we give up. It's great that you can take notes, so you don't miss anything important.

When you overcome a difficult situation, you feel accomplished. You look back at how you felt during that time and realize that you just knew it had to happen, and now you can move forward. What was your mindset during that time? Did you think, "I can do this," or did you have a different strategy? Whatever it was, you were determined to make it work.

I want you to describe in detail how did you feel when you accomplish things? How did it make you feel inside? Were you happy, fulfilled, ecstatic, over the moon, feeling unstoppable? Did you feel the world was your oyster? Anything is possible! Where did that leave you? Where did that pull you? How did looking in the mirror at yourself make you feel about yourself? When you went to bed that night, did you prop yourself up with a pillow and think to yourself, 'Hey, you know what? I'm pretty good. I got through that. Cool.'

You had to decide, even if there were people helping you. You still had to make the final decision. You still had to show up, you still had to get through that really difficult moment. When you learned how to walk, you fell first. If you learned how to ride a bicycle, you fell off the bike first. When you even took a breath, you had to learn how to breathe. Even if you have disabilities, there is a reason you're here. Nick, I can't think of his last name now, is a big motivational speaker.

He was born with no arms and no legs. He tried to take his life at I think eight years old. He tried to drown himself in the tub. As he grew up, his mother wanted to make things harder for him so that he wouldn't feel treated differently. She made him climb on a chair to reach the cookies, instead of putting them easily within his reach. She believed that this would help him face challenging situations in life.

If you google him, you will find him. He's a beautiful man. He's married and has children. He lives an active life and goes scuba diving and fishing. He has an absolutely incredible life. He visits schools and teaches students about self-worth and self-esteem. He teaches young girls to be true to themselves and to love their bodies. He teaches young men the same thing. He is inspirational. When you examine this, you can see how someone learned to overcome a tough situation.

If you're more fortunate than him, you're already a step ahead. What did he have to go through? The thing is, where does his state have to be to do that? What does his story have to be? Look at the strategies that he could create? How does he feel when he's done? He is helping people feel good. I want you to describe in detail how you feel when you have accomplished something good. Tell me why you want to get into real estate? Why now? Why is this a must for you? Get crystal clear on this. This will determine your success.

One way to help yourself is to find an accountability partner to stay on track with the wholesale program instead of getting distracted by social media.

Maybe there's someone who wants to learn with you. I want you to ask yourself these questions. Why do you want to get into real estate? Why did you choose wholesaling? Why did you choose this program? Why now? Write down some information about your current situation in terms of your economic, financial, spiritual, and physical state. Write down details about your employment status and how the current state of the economy, whether it's pre-COVID, during COVID, or post-COVID, has affected you? I'm also curious to know why you are looking for an opportunity like this right now. It would be great if you could write down these details.

Why is this so important to you? I want to emphasize that it became crystal clear to me that this was going to be my everything. When I got my first real estate coach, I was tired of doing one deal at a time and going from one property to another. It was a painful process, and I had enough of it. That's why I took action and got off my nail. It was time for a change.

When I was younger, I felt that real estate was a necessity for me because I had seen what having factory jobs was doing to my parents. They were often in bad moods because of various reasons. I can relate to them because if I don't get to see my husband when I want to, I too feel upset. Whatever stage of life you are in, there is always something that drives you. If you are ready to take your real estate investing to the next level, you can join me for one-on-one coaching. With my guidance, you can go further and faster than on your own. This way, you can save money on costly mistakes that you might make otherwise.

I just wanted to let you know that our one-on-one coaching program is available. It's a comprehensive wholesale package that includes everything I know. I'll teach you all the modules, and when you're ready, we can discuss one-on-one coaching to take you to the next level.

Chapter 2

I want to make sure that you got your Chapter 1 assignments completed, that you wrote out the answers and took that chapter seriously. It's important to understand what you want in detail. Write down the reasons behind why you want those things or experiences. It's crucial to gain clarity on this. We talked about stories, families, friends, and opportunities. Write down why they are important to you. Identify the emotions and feelings associated with them. During the chapter, we discussed your state. Write down what you learned about it. Did you realize that you have a negative attitude sometimes? Or did you discover that you usually feel good about yourself and have a positive attitude? Also, write down what you learned about your story. Did you notice how it affects your state? Or did you realize that your state can dictate the story you tell yourself?

I really need you to get crystal clear on this. I strongly suggest that once you write all of this down, put it somewhere where you can see it, whether it's a reminder on your phone, on your wall, on your dream board, wherever it is, but you want to look at it and refer to it often.

How do we determine where to start our real estate wholesaling business? Do we randomly pick a location, or is it based on a place we have visited in the past, a place we want to retire to, our hometown, or a nearby city? Or is it in another country altogether? We need to evaluate our options before proceeding.

When determining the best market for wholesaling, it requires taking emotions out of real estate investing. Cute features or a property that needs work are not reasons to acquire it, but they don't rule a property out either. My goal is to help you find the best market so that you can make a profit. Choose a city you want to target.

The first thing to do is go to or call the city planning department and ask what their five-year plan is for that area. Are there any new developments? Are there multi-units being built? Are there more single-family homes being built? Are there more conversions? Are there more condos or more townhouses? Find out what's going on in the area that you're thinking about wanting to start your wholesale business in. Is there a demand for rental properties? Is the demand for 2 units, 4 units, or 20 units or more? Know that dialogue. You want to know what's going on. You want to know what their plan is for the next five years, even for the next year.

If you are looking to understand a city at a deeper level, even if you have lived there your whole life, it is important to know what has been happening in the last five years. Just because you are familiar with town gossip or know the corner store owner who retired, it doesn't mean you have knowledge about the city's planning. For choosing your marketplace, understanding the town gossip is not as important as knowing the city's current affairs, or someone working in the planning department. It's important for you to stay informed about the latest developments in marketing. This knowledge will come in handy when you're speaking with potential buyers, as you'll be able to provide them with accurate information and statistics. By staying up to date on marketing trends and developments, you can confidently discuss the past, present, and future of the industry and make informed decisions for your business. If I know that there is a high demand for rentals. It is important to keep this in mind and note any information the city provides regarding this matter. It would be wise to stay informed about the current situation.

It is good to know if they are anticipating any immigrants. Are the homes near a hospital or near one of the best schools? Do you know what types of schools are nearby? Are the homes near places of worship? You want to know if the homes are in a class A, B or C location? How many immigrants are they anticipating coming into that area in the next one to five years or more?

Here is the big golden nugget question: what is the highest and best use for properties in this area in that city? What is the biggest thing going on right now? Their response could be the biggest thing going on right now are single-family homes, multi-family-homes, condos, townhouses, commercial storefronts. It is good to know what is going on because knowledge isn't power, action is. However, without knowledge, you don't know which action to take. You don't want to get into wholesaling in an area that you know nothing about. There are so many wholesalers that I've talked to, and I've dealt with and when I have asked them if they have ever visited the city where the property is located, they usually answer with a no. When I am wholesaling a contract and a Cash Buyer asks me why they should invest in that area, I feel it is my duty and my obligation to tell them everything I know about the area and what is up and coming.

What I'm really recommending and encouraging you to do is to imagine that your mother or your children will live on that property in that city. You should know everything that's going on around the area. What schools are nearby? Are there city buses available? What jobs are available in the area? Where will she go shopping? What is she going to do? What is the average household income? Therefore, it's crucial to take a vested interest in knowing everything about that area. This way, you can bring all the information to the table.

As you talk to more people, you become better informed. You can ask better questions, which leads to a better understanding of the situation. When you approach conversations with a mindset of wanting to learn and know more, you can ask questions like, "Tell me more" or "What else can you tell me?" You can also inquire about who else might provide insight, such as the permit department. Specifically, you can ask about what permits have been issued in the last six months, who is building where, and what's happening in the area. You can also do research on Google, House Sigma, or Zillow to gather more information about the city and its surroundings. It's recommended to start with the city's planning department because they have the most accurate and reliable information about the area. They're responsible for tracking the city's growth and development, so they're the best source of factual information.

Your first assignment is to call or go to the city you want to target. I highly recommend that you do not continue to the next lesson until you've done this. It's so important to not skip and rush through. Some people want to fast-track and show results quickly, but whether you're a first-time real estate buyer or not, it's important to understand the basics. Consider this question: what is the first thing that needs to be built in a new house, the roof, or the foundation? The answer is the foundation—right? It's essential to have a solid foundation before you can build anything else. You might think I don't want to do this; I already know. I'm giving you these little golden nuggets that will bring everything together. I promise you, by the end of this book, everything is going to make sense. Right now, you may look at this puzzle and see scattered pieces. You're wondering how they all fit together. Perhaps, when you were in school, you questioned the relevance of subjects like math and English, thinking, "Why do I need to learn this? I'll just use a calculator or Google."

I just want to let you know that all I'm writing is for your benefit, and you can trust me on this. If there was a way to fast track your progress, it would be in my best interest because I would like to coach you further. My goal is to get you into my masterminds and one-on-one coaching sessions, and I believe you have what it takes to get there. Do your research before you proceed, so you are well-informed.

As we go thru these next chapters, you are going to be talking to more people. Yes, you are going to talk with a lot of people. This business requires you to be outgoing and communicative. Don't be afraid to put yourself out there and engage with people. Everything that I am telling you has a purpose and will come together in the end. Take it step-by-step and follow the course as it is designed. Make calls, network, and get to know people as you go. Trust me, it will all make sense, eventually.

In the next chapter, you will identify who you need to network with and who you're going to talk to besides the city planner. If you're looking for information about the real estate market in a specific location, it's best to contact local realtors as it's their job to keep up with the latest developments. You can ask them questions such as "What's happening in the city that would interest an investor like me?" Inquire about their experience in the field, such as how long they've been licensed, their background before becoming a real estate agent, and whether they're a broker or an agent. Brokers have a team of agents and usually have more knowledge about the market because of their extensive dealings with multiple clients.

Is this real estate agent among one of the top five performers in their office? If this person is the top listing agent, is listing easy? If you want to list your house for sale, all you have to do is find someone interested and ask if they want to sell it. If they do, you can sign the paperwork. Please note that I am not criticizing real estate agents, as they provide valuable services in the industry. I'm just saying, getting a listing is easy. However, selling that property and becoming the buyer's representative on the transaction is different. You have to bring the buyer to the table and have a way about you to make the deal come together. It takes a certain state of mind and skill to meld everything together and make the transaction successful.

When you're the selling agent, and you're one of the top five performers in your office, that's where you know where the people are. You've got a pulse on what's going on. You will want to ask them do you sell residential and or commercial, because it matters. I would recommend with wholesaling we start off with a single-family home. It is nice and simple, and you can get your feet wet. When evaluating commercial properties, it's important to determine if they are multifamily or mixed-use properties, storefronts, or plazas.

It's important to understand the specializations of different real estate agents. For instance, if you're interested in single-family homes and the agent specializes in multi-family properties, it may not be the right fit. It's important to find an agent who is aligned with your goals and understands that you're a wholesaler. You put properties under contract and sell the contract to an investor buyer. Asking that agent if they have clients looking for below market value properties to purchase. For now, the goal is to keep things simple and help you acquire your first or next property with ease.

It is important to ask what city the real estate agent is licensed in because they could live in one city and then be licensed in another state or province. You will need to ask the real estate agent if they get access to off-market deals. This means that they're not listed on the multiple listing services such as realtor.com or realtor.ca websites. Nobody knows about them, besides that realtor. Here are the things you want to know: who do you know that needs to sell fast or who wants an off-market deal, and what is the average number of days single-family homes stay on the market?

Days on market refers to the duration between the time a property is listed and when it's sold. The shorter the days on the market, the more likely it is that it's a seller's market. This means that properties are selling quickly and not staying in the market for long. If a property stays on the market for 90 days or more, it may indicate a slower market with less demand. Now, suddenly, it's a buyer's market. If the buyers are not interested in the property, it can stay on the market a very long time.

This is good information to know because when you're wholesaling and the days on market are too high, it's going to be a struggle to move that property along to a buyer as well. Is the real estate agent a property manager as well? Now, sometimes, someone can be a real estate agent or a property manager. You can ask them if they have any listings with a tired landlord, even if it's a single-family home. The owner might be out of state or province, but not out of the country. They might be out of the city, and as a result, they could be more motivated to sell the property.

So, it's worth asking if they have any such listings. Maybe they have a landlord that is tired of the turnover of tenants. You want to find the pain point as well. You're going to be coming to the local realtors pretty much on two avenues. One is going to be coming from, you're looking to put properties under contract, but then you're also coming from a place of as you're asking the questions do they have any buyers as well, because you may find another source of a property and find your own motivated seller. Now you want to return to that realtor and say, do you have a buyer for this? When talking to real estate agents, there are two important things to discuss. Firstly, you can ask them to send you listings that have been on the market for over 90 days. This is because when a property has been on the market for a long time, its value usually decreases.

For example, if they're asking $200,000, and it's been on the market for 90 days, the chances are it's now worth $150,000, maybe $125,000 or less. The price definitely comes down with that. The other thing is if it's been on the market that long, the owners are very anxious. There's a reason they want to sell the property, and chances are that reason didn't go away. They want that property to move as well. Keep in mind that you want to really negotiate on those. The reason you want to ask for those listings is because there now might be a possibility that the seller is going to work with you on the price or closing date. You never know what opportunity will arise. If it needs more work, the seller may be more motivated to work with your offer. Ask the realtor if they know a good property manager.

If the person you are speaking to is not a property manager, you can ask them if they have any knowledge about the area you are interested in. It is essential to gather as much information as possible about the location you are considering. This way, when you find a potential buyer, you can provide them with all the information they need. For instance, if your buyer is planning to rent out the property, you can recommend a good property manager to help them. Getting to know the area and the people involved in the real estate business can help you make better decisions.

Now that you're facilitating that empire, you're going to become not just the wholesaler, but you're going to become a connector. There is value in being a connector. The more information you have about the investor buyer or the cash buyer, the better. Please understand that your primary objective is to gather information about this city and its real estate market. It's very important that when a buyer contacts you, they find out everything they need to know about the area and why they should invest here. This will also help build trust and a good rapport because it shows them you know your stuff. As you continue to talk to them, you can share your insights and conversations with the city officials and ask for their opinion on it. It's important to look at each city as though YOU were going to buy property there.

You can approach the situation by asking yourself, what do you think is happening in this marketplace? Or what do you believe will happen in this city within the next five years? It's important not to repeat any information you may have heard from the city (unless they gave it to you in writing) that is not public knowledge. The planning department will always have the final say. As a real estate agent tells you about the area, you can use your own judgement. If the agent emphasizes the area's growth and development, you might invest in it.

The city may tell you they have no plans for immigration. There are no immigrants coming in the next five years, there's no growth, there are no new permits. We are in a depressed economy. They might say there is no development in this area. Now you're believing them over a realtor. It seems like the realtor is just getting you to buy property. There are some things you should know about the situation.

You don't want to be like some other wholesalers; it drives me crazy. But what some wholesalers do is they simply turn around and say to a motivated seller, "Great, we'll put your house under contract" and that's it. It doesn't mean that they're going to find a buyer. They don't even know what's going on in that city and you can't even have a conversation with them about the house because they hardly know anything. They can't even tell me anything. As an investor, that's frustrating. I just want to do deals. Just provide me with the facts, including numbers and binary answers, and we'll be ready to proceed. We don't care about the hoopla or colored paperwork. We want the facts. This is precisely what investors are looking for.

Do you know a reliable contractor? In case the realtor sends you a property that requires substantial repairs, it's advisable to ask them if they know a contractor who can handle the job efficiently. You may also request them to recommend someone who can provide quotes for fixing the roof, flooring, foundation, kitchen, or bathroom upgrade, or any other structural issues. It's essential to know the estimated cost of the repairs, and a recommended contractor can help you with that. So, could you please suggest someone reliable for the job?

Realtors and wholesalers have two different ways of doing business. Realtors put the seller under contract to sell their property for a small percentage of the sale price, while wholesalers focus on putting properties under contract at a price below market value and then selling the contract to other investors for a profit. Despite their differences, realtors and wholesalers can be friends and work together. It is important to understand the different roles of the parties involved in a real estate transaction. The seller's agent's primary goal is to sell the property for the highest possible price, while the buyer's agent's primary responsibility is to negotiate the best deal for their client.

A wholesaler acts as a middleman between the seller and the buyer and is looking for an opportunity to make a profit by finding a property that they can put under contract at a higher price than they acquired it for. As a wholesaler, it is crucial to ensure that there is a significant difference between the purchase price and the sale price, and to educate the investor buyer on the potential benefits of the deal. Essentially, a wholesaler works on behalf of both the seller and the buyer to secure a property at a discounted price.

You want to still have a discount to pass on to your buyer. That's where the money is. That's where the juice is. Are you familiar with any real estate attorneys? Have you come across a title company? These two entities will be essential for successfully closing your transaction. The real estate attorney will draft up all the paperwork for your offer to purchase when you are wholesaling and ensure that you are protected when putting the seller under contract. Once that is done, you can assign the contract and proceed with the transaction.

If you have questions about real estate matters such as contracts and wholesaling, it's best to seek advice from a professional real estate attorney. They can assist you in understanding the contract and help explain to you that you'll be wholesaling the property, not buying it. For closing a transaction, the attorney, or title company, plays a crucial role. It is advisable to contact at least three and have a conversation with them. You need to confirm if the buyer can use the same attorney's office as you or the same title company as you once you sell your contract. This will ensure a smooth and hassle-free process of closing the deal.

To ensure a smooth process when dealing with real estate, communicate with the real estate attorney and title company. This will help you stay on top of things and avoid any potential issues. To be successful in the real estate industry, you need to put in effort. This includes making more phone calls, meeting more people, and gaining knowledge about what you're doing. Reach out to real estate attorneys in your area and learn about the market and the rules that apply to your specific location. It's essential to ensure that all your actions are legal and ethical. To make sure you're on the right track, hire an attorney and tell them you are wholesaling and ask for their legal advice on how to proceed with the legal contracts for a successful transaction.

Are you aware of any reliable lenders? In case your buyer requires financing, it's essential to find a few, namely credit unions, mortgage brokers, private lenders, and hard money lenders. Similarly, if your buyer needs insurance for the property, do you know any insurance brokers? It's also a good idea to get in touch with an accountant, especially if you plan on venturing into wholesaling. An accountant can guide you on how to maintain your books and whether you need an LLC, a corporation, or just stay as a sole proprietor. It's crucial to get referrals from realtors and other professionals in the industry and expand your network to include everyone you might need to work with.

What are the fees to sell a single-family home? Suppose you want to close on the property and decide to sell it with a realtor. In that case, asking what fees they will charge is important. It's always good to know what's going on, especially if there's a great deal on the line.

Do you have experience dealing with investors? Some realtors may not have experience working with investors. They are usually used to working with investor buyers who purchase houses to live in. Investors like to buy properties creatively, using techniques like wholesaling and seller financing options. So, it's fair to ask the realtor if they have experience dealing with investors. Another question to ask is if they are open to submitting low-priced offers on your behalf.

Realtors have an ethical obligation to present any buyer offers to the seller, but the seller can refuse. However, I always like to start off with, are you open to doing that? And if they're not, you can do basically one of two things. You can simply reply with 'Oh, okay. Thank you very much' and not submit the offer. Alternatively, you could inform them that rejecting my offer might be a disservice to their seller, as they do not know if the seller will accept my offer.

A lot of times a deal will die, because of the realtor. The realtor can come out and say, don't do this deal. If you have a realtor who is familiar with assignments, they can help. I have experience working with investors and I am familiar with the discounted offers. With me on board, you have a better chance of making money through wholesaling. I can work with this realtor to put through offers on your behalf, which is a great opportunity. I am keen to know if you have any investment property.

It is recommended to contact three real estate agents and ask them a list of questions to better understand the property and the market. You could ask them the questions discussed below.

How long have you been living in this city? Maybe they just migrated to this area from another state, country, city, or province. I want to know what they know about this city, so when I ask why I should invest here and they say it's great, I can gauge their level of familiarity. For instance, if they have only been here for three months, it's not enough time to know the ins and outs of the city. I have talked to realtors who have only been in the country for six months, and they don't have enough knowledge about the city. When I ask how long they've been living here, their answer brings into question their familiarity with the city.

What makes investing in this city so attractive? Why did you choose to become a realtor here? What is it about this city that you love? I am curious about the market situation and what else is happening in the city, beyond the planning department. Do you know any appraisers? They could help me determine the current value of a property. I understand appraisers charge for their services, but it would be helpful to have that information. Also, do you know any inspectors who could help me inspect a property? Your help would be appreciated.

Ask them if they know any home inspectors? An inspector is a person who conducts a safety check on the house. They usually take a lot of pictures and inspect various parts of the house, including the roof, foundation, electrical and plumbing systems, and furnace and central air conditioning systems. They may also provide information about the life expectancy of these systems, the cost of repairs, and even refer some professionals for the job.

You want to know a good inspector, because if you're buying a property or you're wholesaling a property, keep in mind you want to know what the condition of that property is. There are a lot of financing option strategies and seller financing is 1 of them. A seller financing offer is simply asking the seller if they will hold a mortgage. Rather than going to the bank for 90% of the purchase price instead, you're going to go to the seller and ask them to become the bank.

This can only work if the seller has no mortgage or any monies owing on the property. If the seller doesn't owe any money on the property, you can offer them 7% for five years instead of going to the bank for financing. If you partner up with someone who has experience presenting seller financing offers, or if the property is listed with a realtor and that realtor is experienced with seller financing, the seller will be more understanding and supportive during negotiation discussions. This will help you come to an agreement that benefits both you and the seller.

A wholesaler that has some experience in this can explain it to the listing agent and to the seller. It is important to get someone that has experience in this. They know what they're doing, and it makes life a lot easier. If it's a knowledgeable realtor, I am happy because I don't have to train the realtor. I don't want to teach the realtor how to do this stuff. It's too complicated. Maybe I used the wrong word. It's not that the situation is complicated. It's just that I need to explain it clearly to them, hoping that they will understand and be able to explain it in the future. Unfortunately, I won't be present at the next meeting, where it will be just the seller and their realtor. Therefore, it's crucial that I leave a clear explanation for them.

If they're already not versed in that, then there could be a breakdown in communication, which could scare the seller and because of that they say, no, I don't want to do this. And then the deal dies there. Do you have any pocket listings? Pocket listings are exclusive listings that only a specific real estate agent has. All that means is that it hasn't hit the wide market yet. It's listed, however, only they know about it. The office may be the only one that knows about it. You want to find out about those because those can be superb deals. Those are the ones that are kept for their best VIP investors.

What are your office hours? There's this one place I needed to contact, but I don't even know their Friday hours. Sometimes I try calling after 2:30 p.m. but can't reach anybody. So, I want to know what are your office hours, not just your location, but what hours are you available? Are you a morning person or a night owl? Do you prefer phone calls, text messages, or emails? I want to know what works best for you because I need answers quickly. I want to move fast and scale my work, so it's important for me to know how quickly you usually respond. I understand you can be busy with appointments or showings, but what's your usual response time? Is it within an hour, 24 hours, or longer? Also, what are your business days and hours?

If you're interested in getting to know someone who shares your interests, or if you're working a full-time job and want to pursue wholesaling as a side hustle, it's essential to find a realtor who is available after 5 p.m. or on weekends. This will help you work around your schedule and ensure that you can collaborate with the realtor effectively. It's crucial to find a realtor who can work with you at a convenient time so that you can build a solid partnership.

It is recommended to contact several real estate agents until you find the one who you can work well with. Let them know you are an investor who is interested in purchasing the property either for yourself or for one of your investor buyers. The property should have a value-added opportunity that you can take advantage of. Inform them you will submit offers and negotiate accordingly. If I cannot close on a property myself, I plan to assign it to one of my investor buyers. I have a list of such buyers and if I am not interested, I can easily find someone who is. I will inform the seller beforehand that this is how I conduct my business, so there are no surprises later.

In the end, it is important that they understand the need for added value and that you're not looking for turnkey properties. Now, with that being said, you could look for that and we'll get into that further on in the lessons. What a buyer wants, however, is the potential to increase the value of a property because you can't change the location no matter what you do. Maybe it needs a bit of work or an upgrade, or its current zoning can be changed, or the land can be severed because it is such a large lot, or it's a corner lot. These factors play a HUGE role. However, it's important to communicate to the realtor that you're not just looking for cookie-cutter deals, but for something that has value and potential. There must be a value added that justifies buying the property, because that's what your investor buyers will look for-opportunities and good deals. Therefore, it's crucial to be clear with the realtor about what you're looking for, so you can both be on the same page.

Contact appraisers in the local area. When speaking with them, I recommend you inquire about their fees and the turnaround time for receiving the report. You'll also want to ensure that the appraisers take multiple photos of the property. These reports can be lengthy, ranging from 20 to 60 pages. You could ask them how quickly they can deliver the report. We need to look at the comparable properties in the area and determine the value of the property.

You could check if they know any motivated sellers. They are in many people's properties regularly, so perhaps they come across someone who needs to sell their house urgently. The homeowner might say, "I need to get rid of this house. I can't take it anymore." The person working on the property might know someone who can help. All they have to say is, "Can you give them my number?" They could even have a card ready with your name and phone number and ask the homeowner to call you. Can you recommend any contractors? How long have they been licensed? You want someone who's reputable in that city. If you're a wholesaler from out of town and you're going to be doing business in a new city, don't be afraid to get to know the locals. You'll be relying on them, so it's important to build relationships.

You want to ensure that you have complete knowledge about the people you are dealing with so that they can make up for what you don't know. It's important to know how long they have been in business and if they hold any licenses. Perhaps the person you are referring to had multiple professions? They were an electrician or a plumber or a real estate agent before, but it's difficult to say for sure. If you want to know more, you could ask them if they hold any other licenses or what accreditations they have. Also, it's important to clarify whether they offer both residential and commercial services or just specialize in one. If you're looking for a residential appraiser for a single-family home, it's best to go for someone who specializes solely in residential properties.

If the appraiser offers both residential and commercial services, it may cause higher costs and longer turnaround times. Can you confirm if the appraisal includes an after-repair value assessment besides the current as-is assessment? The as-is appraisal determines the current value of the property in its existing condition. The after-repair value appraisal determines the value of the property once it has been updated and improved to its highest and best use, with additions like an extra dwelling unit. If updates were made to the property, such as upgrading the bathroom and kitchen, painting the house, and cleaning it up, what would be the value of the property then?

What we need to do is ask the appraiser if they would provide an after-repair value appraisal. This will help us determine the property's value after the necessary repairs are done. Many appraisers do not provide this appraisal, but it is crucial for investors and investor buyers. For instance, if the as-is appraisal is $200,000 and the after-repair appraisal is $300,000, we could put an offer on the property for $150,000, assign the contract for $180,000, making a profit of $30,000 on a wholesale deal with a motivated seller who sells for $150,000. By offering to sell the contract of the property under the as is value, the buyer knows they are getting a good deal. They are getting equity the moment they buy the property.

The after-repair value is $300,000. Now, suddenly, the buyer is saying, "Wait a minute, I know what my profit margin is. I will make this much on this deal, and I will make that much on that deal." The key is to present them with facts. What you say doesn't matter as much as the documentation you provide. When you're considering gaining a property, it's important to ask the appraiser how much they charge for each appraisal. I highly recommend getting both appraisals, even if you ultimately decide not to go through with the deal. It's a worthwhile investment in the long run. It is also a write-off that you could discuss with your accountant. It's recommended to always do everything you can do to check if it's a good deal that would require your time, not your money.

It's highly recommended that you keep in mind that most wholesalers do not provide an appraisal to the investor buyer, so you should be careful before making any purchase decisions.

They do not provide an *as is,* nor do they apply an ARV appraisal. You're suddenly marketing yourself above the other wholesalers. Wholesalers are a dime a dozen. I get at least 30 to 50 wholesalers emailing me every day with leads or so-called deals. I can tell you that every time I replied to them, I asked if they had an appraisal or an inspection. However, their response was always a *nope.* This made me realize that I would have to go through the trouble of finding an appraisal and inspection, as they wanted me to close the deal in just 10 days. This lack of preparation on their part is stopping me from being able to move forward.

As an investor buyer, I might request an independent appraisal, but your appraisal still provides me with a starting point. It's useful to have your appraisal to refer to and see what you've done. I've put some effort into this transaction. I ended up putting some money into the transaction. Now I know there's a reason to move forward. You could ask the appraisers about their previous experience and what they were doing before? It would be helpful to know which city they are currently working in, and whether they live in the same city where they perform appraisals. Also, please inquire about their availability. Some appraisers might be too busy to attend the property immediately, so it's better to clarify their availability beforehand. Knowing all these details will help us get a better understanding of their work and availability.

You are curious about the expectation when you make a deal with a seller and need to get an appraiser within a tight timeframe of five days to remove conditions and complete the deal. This can cause a delay, and you want to be aware of any such risks beforehand. Be aware of that and call local inspectors. Ask them questions, take a lot of pictures, ask how much they charge and ask how quickly you can get a report? The report should be more detailed than an appraiser's report. It should include pictures of the electrical panel, any cracks in the foundation, holes in the roof, plumbing drips, broken windows, and old wiring in the property. They should also tell the type of wiring, plumbing, and even the age of the property or the roof. They should inform them if the venting has been taken care of properly. They should tell you if there is mold on the property. They will also point out if ceiling beams have been taken out. These are things I've experienced over the years. You will want to find out how quickly they can get a report to you.

You need to ask them if they have any information regarding potential motivated sellers? The same question goes for appraisers and inspectors, as they often visit people's homes and may come across someone who cannot afford repairs. In such cases, you can tell them please share my contact information with the motivated seller. Ask them do they know any contractors? Inspectors are often tasked with finding issues, but they may also provide solutions, much like contractors. Ask them how long you have been in business and if they hold any licenses. Ask what profession they had before becoming an inspector. Ask if they own rental properties or are an investor in the city. Inquire about the timeline for property availability.

You can ask them how soon you can see the property? This is crucial, as any delays in inspection could cause a missed opportunity. You want to be sure that the property inspector is available and can act promptly. If the inspector has a backlog, it's best to call another one. Most likely 99.9% of wholesalers don't get an inspection for the investor buyer. All I'm suggesting is that if you're selling a property, disclose all the issues with it to the buyer. This way, they will know exactly what they're getting into. If the sale falls through, you can claim the expenses on your taxes. For example, let's say you negotiate a deal for $150,000, and you pay for an inspector to evaluate the property. If the inspector finds 50 problems with it, disclose this to the investor buyer. They may still want to buy the property, but at least they know what they're getting into. And if the sale falls through, you can write off the expenses on your taxes. Just confirm this with your accountant.

Now you can go back to the seller and say, "Hey, I know I offered you $150,000, but based on these problems with your property, I need to review this number. I can't do $150,000, but I can do $100,000." That gives you bargaining power with the seller, and suddenly they may agree. Keep in mind that when you have the appraiser come in, they won't look into every detail and issue with the property. Their focus is to determine the as-is value of the property. They will take a general look around the property and make a note of any significant issues that may affect the value. They will also consider the value of other properties in the neighborhood that were recently sold. This information will help them reach a fair and accurate appraisal of the property.

They are going to pay attention to the lot size to match the recently sold lots in the area. As they do that, the appraiser will come up with a value for the property. If the value is $200,000, which is likely, you can use the inspection as leverage to negotiate a lower purchase price. However, keep in mind that the appraisal and inspection will be based on the property's current condition. When you speak to the appraiser, you can tell them that based on their findings, what needs to be improved to reach an excellent condition. If you can make these improvements, then ask them what the property's worth will be after repair value (ARV).

Now the appraiser will come and evaluate the property from a different perspective. If he values it at $300,000, you can see the potential profit. If you buy it for $100,000 as is, you could assign that contract for $200,000 and then your investor buyer could sell it again for $300,000 after improvements. It's important to understand the end goal and purpose behind this strategy. I hope this helps in expanding your knowledge and understanding of the process.

The inspection report is being used twice, once to negotiate with the seller and the other one to show the investor buyer the things that need to be done. Inspectors will examine various aspects of a property, and investors will review the inspection report to identify potential issues. Typically, investors focus on five key areas: the roof, foundation, plumbing, electrical wiring, and the HVAC system. Other details in the report are important for investors to understand the overall condition of the property.

When presenting an inspection report to someone, it's important to consider the purpose behind it. Some may feel overwhelmed by the expenses that may arise from the report, but it's essential to assess the situation and determine if you have the crew, contractors, and staff to handle it. It's going to cost you some money. I'm teaching you the difference between throwing money away and investing. Investing involves some costs, like doing your own research and due diligence. It's better if you can get pictures of the property and figure out if it's worth it. For instance, if the house is dilapidated, it may not be wise to invest in it when you are first starting this wholesaling journey.

You may not want to make an offer, which means you may skip the inspection and appraisal. To be successful in real estate, a lot of effort is required in making phone calls, visiting properties, and thoroughly understanding the market conditions. It is recommended to reach out to your bank branch manager and ask about the buyers in the area to get a better understanding of the market trends. Do you know the buyers in the area? Are buyers struggling to qualify? How many buyers are there? What are the current interest rates? Are they increasing or decreasing?

You want to know if buyers in that area are actively searching for properties. Is there a lot of movement? Are they seeing a lot of offers come across their desk? Are they getting a lot of offers approved? Those are some things you want to ask them about. Find the top producing real estate companies in three different firms and observe their activities. Ask them if they have buyers with cash now. If they're the selling agents, then that means that they know people. Do you know anyone who is looking? You might have future wholesale deals to share with them.

Please find out what the criteria is for their buyers. What is their purchase price? How much can they afford? What's the sweet spot? Is it $200,000? Is it $400,000? Is it a million? What does that look like? I love this question. Is it a buyer's or a seller's market? If it's a buyer's market, then things are going to sit longer. It is important that you negotiate a better price for the contract, otherwise you may not sell it. You need to be prepared for higher property prices if you are buying in a seller's market. When buying a property in a market, it is important to understand the type of market you are in. In a seller's market, there are fewer properties available for sale and the demand is high. In this scenario, as a buyer, you may need to negotiate harder to get a good deal. However, in a buyer's market, there are more properties available for sale and the demand is low. This gives you a better chance of negotiating down the price and getting a good deal.

When it's a seller's market, it means that there's not a lot of inventory on the market. It means that the sellers will probably get a higher value for their property and that's the position you want to be in, a seller's market. Besides this, know that there are motivated sellers that don't really care about the sale price because they need to move on quickly or the house is in rough shape. A sellers' market is what investors are excited about because they buy, fix and sell for quicker profits.

Your assignment is to call three appraisers, three inspectors, three realtors, and three city branch managers. I would strongly suggest you don't move on until you've done this. You want to make sure that you've got a handle on what's going on. You want to ensure that you are well-informed about the current situation of the properties in different locations. To achieve this, you need to connect with people who have knowledge about the cost, timelines, and whether it is a buyer's or seller's market. Having a pulse of these factors would be beneficial in making informed decisions.

Again, I strongly suggest you do this assignment. Chapter 3 is about how to reach thousands of cash buyers. Making money depends on selling the contract. This is where it gets interesting. I hope to keep you engaged by emphasizing networking and opportunities, leading to cash buyers.

You are looking for a way to build a buyer's list in a particular city. One effective method is to post on social media platforms like Facebook, Instagram, TikTok, and LinkedIn, stating that you are interested in building a buyer's list and looking for cash buyers in that city. Ask them to DM you with their email address, so you can add them to your list. This method can help you gradually add interested buyers to your list.

The reality of it is, with no buyers for those contracts, you will not make any money wholesaling. So we've got to go out now and we've got to go hunt. Look where the cash buyers are. Meet with your hairstylist or barber and ask them about the local real estate market. Let them know you are interested in buying a property with cash. Hairstylists often have a lot of good information because they chat with many people while doing their job. When you go to the salon, you can start a conversation with your stylist about their life, where they live, and what they do. In this way, you can gather a wealth of information. I often give my business cards to hairstylists, and I even offer them a referral fee if they refer a successful lead to me. This could be $100, $500, or even a ticket to Hawaii. They are so valuable because they know what's happening in the local real estate market.

Hair stylists are privy to a lot of information. For instance, they are aware of who is selling or buying a property, the latest gossip in town, and even upcoming permits that the city may not yet know about. Surprisingly, realtors may not always be knowledgeable about these matters. They're really at the heart of it. Tell them you are a cash buyer. Now you might think, I'm not a cash buyer, I don't have any money, I can assure you that if you find a deal and you put it under contract, you're going to find cash, people will come out of the woodwork to throw money at you if you have a deal.

Many people think that raising capital or getting cash is the hardest part of the deal. It's really not. It's getting a deal. If you get a deal, the money will come. If you don't have a deal, there is no money coming. No one's going to want to invest in a sinking ship. You should tell them you get deals all the time and give them your contact info. You will have more opportunities when you tell them you are both a buyer and seller. Do you want to become the go-to hairstylist for your clients? If so, it's important to build strong relationships with them and make sure they feel comfortable and valued.

If someone's approaching me to sell their property, I'm not paying retail value. I can pay retail value with the listed property all day long. If you're going to come to me and you need to sell quickly and it's in despair, then it's going to be at my price on my terms, and I may make that known openly.

If you decide to pawn something at a pawnshop, be aware that they will most likely offer you much less than what your item is worth. For example, if you pawn a diamond ring from a past relationship, they may only offer you 10 cents on the dollar. They won't tell you the true value of the ring and offer you something close to that. Instead, they will say that the most they can offer you is $10, $20, or $30. So, it's important to keep this in mind before deciding to pawn something valuable.

My perspective is that I am like a pawnshop for real estate. I'm just moving real estate. Other people are moving gold, or tools, etc. All I'm doing is moving real estate contracts, and I'm just getting it from the seller to the buyer as quickly as possible. I want to make money in between and create the opportunity and create the deal. There might not be a deal on the surface. The realtor might not even know that there's a deal there. Maybe the seller didn't disclose that. I've had sellers reach out to me on properties that were listed and negotiate a lower price than what was listed. The realtor sometimes can be the ones that are stopping a deal without intentionally or unintentionally doing that.

Find out their criteria and save their emails. With bartenders, they know what's happening because they interact with people who are drinking. However, it's important to maintain a professional relationship and not spend too much time socializing with them. I'm just inviting you to look at that and know people at a whole other level. If you want to follow up with potential clients, learn about their needs and preferences. You can keep their contact information and stay in touch with them outside of their work hours. For example, you could chat with a hairdresser, a bartender, or a pawnshop owner after their shift. Share your contact details and ask them the best way to follow up with them, such as via text, call, or email.

It's important to establish a good relationship with potential networking partners. You don't want to come across as annoying, but you do want to show that you're eager to make things happen. Your task is to promote yourself on social media, get a new hairstylist, visit a few pawnshops, and talk to a couple of bartenders. Let them know that you're an investor looking to buy real estate, and that you can close deals quickly.

Don't move on until you do the above. Again, these are little seeds that you have to plant. You've got to know your area and you have to have some buyers. Set your expectations with the cash buyer and let them know you're going to require a minimum $3,000 non-refundable deposit or earnest money deposit (EMD) sent to your lawyer or attorney or a title company within 24 hours. If they're moving forward with the deal and if they can't commit to this, I suggest you remove them from your list. You want people that are serious, you want buyers that are serious, and you want to move these deals. If they can't commit to that, call it a day, especially as we were talking about an appraisal that requires due diligence and inspection to inform a buyer.

When the investor buyer is viewing the property, a non-refundable deposit is required to move forward. If you're concerned about a buyer circumventing you and making a deal directly with the seller, consult your lawyer or attorney. Ask them how you can secure the contract to ensure that the buyer cannot go around you. Your lawyer or attorney will provide you with the documents to protect your interests. It's important to monitor this issue, and lawyers and attorneys are well-equipped to handle it.

Here's a note: if you don't get at least 20 cash buyers within 24 to 72 hours. I recommend changing your location to target more cash buyers in that city. If you're looking to build a buyer's list for a specific city, a great option is to find and join Facebook groups related to that area. You can post on those groups, letting members know that you're looking for buyers in that location.

Don't limit yourself to just your personal Facebook page. Expand your reach by posting on other businesses' pages and networking with other professionals. Get creative with your approach and you'll see positive results. If you want to invest in a particular city, it's important to do your research and find the best opportunities available, especially if the city has a growing market and it's a seller's market. This means that the property is likely to sell quickly, so it's important to act fast. When you are searching for potential buyers, keep in mind the location you are searching in. If you cannot find any buyers, consider changing the location as a hot location should have potential buyers. If there are no buyers, then there is no way to make money.

Facebook Ad Copy to Attract Motivated Sellers

https://app.bitly.com/Bo4pjwghIeQ/http://bit.ly/3WVPihO

Chapter 3

Chapter 3 is all about the sellers and their whereabouts. Where do they live? Where do they hide? Where can we find the sellers of all this real estate? Where are the motivated sellers hanging out? These are some questions we will explore in this chapter. How desperate are they? Find a motivated seller by posting on social media and **drive for dollars**. This is a way to find motivated sellers by driving around and leaving notes on dilapidated properties. Leave a note on the door that says *call me, I buy houses*. Spread the word that you buy houses-have a website and leave notes in mailboxes. Reach out to hairdressers, pawnshops, contractors, inspectors, bank managers, mortgage brokers, and lawyers. Use Google Ads and paid advertising to find potential sellers. They are everywhere, among us-just waiting to be found.

The more people you talk to, the more likely you are to find potential sellers. They may even be on social media, just like you. Keep in mind they may be scared, confused, and anxious, so approach them with care and empathy. The sellers may be desperate, especially if they're losing their property, if they owe money on the property, if they owe back taxes, or if they're under foreclosure. They are confused about who they trust and are going to be reserved and may not want to talk to you right away. That's the thing, a motivated seller is looking for a motivated buyer. They're looking for you. Trust me on that.

If you have thoroughly researched your investor buyers and done your due diligence, you can approach the seller with confidence that you can help them. You know what's going on and you have the buyers for their property. The seller may feel alone and distrustful, but you can assure them you are there to help. It's important to understand that criticism is not personal. It's crucial to focus on the conversation and not take it personally. How much does the property owe in back taxes? How much does the property owe on a mortgage? You never want to ask someone how much they owe on their house when discussing repairs. Don't make it personal. Ultimately, it's about the property, and the more we can separate the property from the person, the better. Our aim is to assist the seller with a problem, which is the need to sell. The property is simply the object that needs to be sold, and that's all we know for sure.

When you're connecting with someone, it's important to empathize with them and understand their feelings. Put yourself in their shoes and think about how you would want to be talked to if you were in their position-scared, unsure, and untrusting. How would you want someone to respond to you if you felt that way? Ask the seller what their situation is, and really feel their pain, their sorrow, their frustration, their anger, their fear. Spend about 45 minutes getting to know them and find common ground. People don't care how much you know; it's how much you care. They really don't care about what you know, but they do care if they feel that you genuinely care about them. You're solving a problem for them. Their problem could be that they have a property they don't want, or they don't want a *For Sale* sign on their lawn because they feel embarrassed about it.

Perhaps some people don't want their curious neighbors to snoop around their property and find out about their personal matters. It's surprising how many deals I get just because some neighbors want to keep their privacy intact and not reveal their activities to others. They don't want to hold open houses, because they don't want people coming through their home. It's important to understand what someone is going through. Finding a lot of common ground builds their trust as well. It is an icebreaker. People only do business with people they know, like, and trust.

Sellers do not know who you are, so it is important to engage with them. Ask them *how can I help you? What's the situation with the property? Why do you need to sell? How soon do you need to sell the property?* Let them know you are a problem solver, and you will help them figure this out for them. When you complete all your homework, you will feel confident while communicating with a seller. This is very important as the seller wants to know that you can solve their problem.

To find out more details, ask more questions. Why do they need to sell? Do you have to sell the property? Do you have a place to go? Where are you going? Are you downsizing? Are you moving to a different city, province, state, or a different country? Are you going away to school or work? Do you understand what's happening with the property owners? It's not really about the property features, such as the number of bedrooms, bathrooms, or square footage, or even the repairs needed. Ultimately, it's about their motivation to sell quickly and become unattached from the property. That's what drives their decision-making process.

It's important to avoid asking someone to tell you about their home directly. Home is a very emotional word and topic, so it's better to ask about the property instead. Distinguishing between the two is crucial. The lesson here is to become their best friend-you should be able to laugh and even cry with them.

Don't judge them, just listen. You do not know what they are going through. It is important to empathize with them. My coach told me I was being judgmental towards people, and I didn't understand why they were behaving the way they were. I argued it wasn't my fault they acted that way, but my coach helped me realize I needed to be more empathetic and less judgmental.

I often tell sellers I'm sorry they're going through a tough time. However, the only way I can help them is by buying their property for a discounted price. Usually, they don't consult a real estate agent to list their property, so negotiating on the price is their only option available.

I always give people the option to consider alternatives before going through with a real estate transaction with me. For instance, I suggest asking if they've contacted a real estate agent or considered investing money in the property to improve its condition. It's important to make them aware of the time frame (90 days) to sell and to consider the potential inconvenience of having multiple people touring the property. Once I've received three to four NOs from a potential client for other options, I become the logical choice to help them sell their property. As a wholesaler, I recognize the value I bring to the value chain by eliminating the need for open houses, real estate commissions, and property repairs.

When you're selling or buying something, it's important to keep in mind what you bring to the table. If you approach potential sellers in an aggressive and salesy manner, they won't be able to hear what you're saying, and they will resist anything you offer them. That's why it's important to approach them from a place of compassion and care. If you show up with your arms crossed and pushy, they'll only hear that and not your message. Remember, you're there to help solve their problems, so approach them with kindness and understanding. This way, you'll have a better chance of sealing the deal quickly.

The reality of it is that they need to get out of their own way. There was a deal we made with an elderly couple. We negotiated the price quite low and took possession of the property as-is.

We put some money in their pocket, and they could move on. We closed this deal. We looked at the plumbing, and we realized they didn't even have running water to their bathroom sink or tub, just for the toilet.

When we tested the water at the well, we found that the water was contaminated. There was also mold in the rooms. By us getting them out of that property, we did them a favor. Sometimes people can get stuck in a difficult situation and can't see a way out. We were able to help these individuals move into a pleasant apartment when no one else was offering any help. Moments like that make us proud of what we do.

When we wholesale deals, it's really amazing. A seller would come on board with us, and we could sell it to a buyer who is thrilled that they could get a house at a lower price than the market rate. We negotiate for a better price, and so we can offer the same house at a lower rate to the buyer. This is a tremendous benefit we can provide to people.

I often encounter situations where the property owners are hesitant to sell their properties. They may have had bad experiences with previous buyers or may be skeptical of new buyers. In such cases, I eliminate their doubts by asking a few questions. I ask them if they have considered listing the property, doing all the repairs to make it look great, and showing it to hundreds of people to sell it on their own. These questions are non-invasive, and I usually ask them over the phone before seeing them in person. By doing so, I hope to make the process smoother and less stressful for everyone involved.

I understand that if I haven't seen the property, then I'm not sure about its condition. It could be a hoarder house or completely dilapidated, but I'm just asking questions. I want to clarify that I do not know about the property whatsoever. If I ask whether the property has been listed or if necessary repairs have been made, it's not meant to be taken personally. Usually, people say they don't want to pay a commission or they don't have the money for repairs. Also, I don't know if the property is in immaculate condition or not. I want to respect people's privacy, so I don't push them to show the property if they don't want to. It's important to understand that people have their reasons for not wanting to allow others inside their homes.

I need to consider the reasons some people may not want to sign a contract with me. If any of these reasons apply to them, then the chances are high that they will prefer to work with someone else rather than with me. Therefore, it's crucial to understand where they are coming from and what they expect. I need to meet them where they are at and understand their perspective to make sure we are on the same page. What are they looking at getting out of this by selling to you? Ask them what is the lowest cash offer they would accept? Ask what they would accept right now. When they respond with a decision, no matter what they say, respond with seriousness. Say seriously, if we close at your preferred time and take care of everything, what is the lowest amount you would take? Seriously, if we closed, that's how I do it. If we agree to close the deal on your terms and take the property as is with no commission, what is the lowest cash offer you would accept?

Also, it's important to ask them what closing date they prefer, as it's not up to me to decide. If your buyers are ready to go, we can close the deal in seven days. Let me know what you think. If they can close the deal quickly, then yes, the closing can happen rapidly. However, the specific closing date they prefer may vary-it could be 30 days or 60 days, for instance. Ultimately, it all depends on what they want. You want to make it about them, you want to meet them where they're at and meet their needs. The more needs that you can meet, the better chance you have of getting this under contract.

To get a better understanding of a situation, it's important to be aware of what's happening behind the scenes. As a dentist, you may need to take on the role of a counselor to help your patients. This may involve asking them questions to figure out what's going on and how you can best assist them. For example, you may need to ask about any outstanding payments owed on their property. It's not about how much you owe, but how much is the property worth and what is owed on it. The problem lies with the property itself, such as missed mortgage payments or unpaid taxes. Therefore, it's important to focus on the property and gather all the details to explore options.

If you're interested in a property, it's important to do your due diligence. One of the first things to consider is the property taxes. You should also take notes on the property, including its lot size and whether it's a corner lot. It's also important to know the zoning of the property. Is it zoned for mixed use, commercial, residential, or multifamily? Be sure to double-check the lot size as well. Sometimes it's easy to mistake the neighboring property's lot size for the property you're interested in, as happened to me once.

If the property is a corner lot, there might be some opportunity there that you wouldn't want to tell the seller. Is there a possibility of severance? Is there a possibility you can make two lots out of that property? Those are some things to consider. When you're looking at the zoning, you're looking at what's the potential of the zoning. Maybe it is zoned so that it can be two units or maybe it can be zoned for four or six units.

You want to find out what they know about their property and prove to them you can solve their problem. Let them know we create win-win scenarios. Explain to them your business model. I like to be upfront. We buy properties at deep discounts; we fix them up to be a plus condition, and we resell them for a profit. Are you okay with that?

Even though you're wholesaling and buying properties at a deep discount, you're only putting the property under contract and telling the seller that either you or another investor will buy the property. You're seeking their permission for this intention. Are you okay with that? There hasn't been anyone that has said to me, *no, I'm not okay with that*. I have had some say, *as long as I'm making money, I don't care*. You should communicate your business model and ensure it benefits both parties. Because if they're not ok with it, we can't proceed. You can give them a letter of intent to sign showing the $100 deposit.

Before setting up the contract, you will need to create a letter of intent. Even though it is not a contractual obligation, it serves to communicate your intention to proceed with the contract. A letter of intent is simply that, it's not a contractual obligation whatsoever. If you're communicating with someone over the phone and need to send them a document, you can email it to them. The document should have your signature on it. Once they receive it, they can sign it using DocuSign and send it back to you. This way, the document will have a record of both signatures. My intention is that we agree on a price and a closing date and establish the conditions for the transaction. Later, we can discuss whether any investors need to view the property before finalizing the deal.

It's a good idea to send a letter of intent to someone after they've agreed to sign, as this helps to solidify their commitment. This letter serves as official documentation of their agreement and can give them peace of mind knowing that the deal is done.

Once you give them the letter of intent to sign, it means that they have committed to the offer. This letter serves as confirmation that you are interested in the property. Your lawyer will also confirm this. The offer amount should be the lowest number that you will pay for the property.

It's not the time really to do a lot of negotiating. You need to do your homework. Do the digging, do the due diligence, and find out what's going on. You can start by checking websites to see what properties in the area are going for. You can also call local realtors and ask them about the city, areas, and locations. When you don't have a property in mind, ask them all the questions you have.

When this seller says to you that their property is at 123 main street you can look at 123 Main Street on the map and see that 123 Main Street is near this, is near that. The realtor mentioned the city had confirmed the details regarding the property. I've talked to some appraisers, inspectors, hairdressers, bartenders, pawnshop owners to research. When you come across 123 Main Street, you can use the knowledge you have stored in your mind to understand the area. You can recall if it's a good or bad location, that's a Class B or class C location, and make informed decisions accordingly.

The letter of intent is allowing you to buy time to do some due diligence, so that you're not just running around getting an appraisal and inspection. It's not about instantly spending money. It's about how quickly you can analyze a situation and decide. Once you've determined that a particular opportunity is worthwhile, contact a lawyer, make an offer, and move on to the next step. The faster that you can get at this stage, the better. That's why it was so important in the previous chapters to help you familiarize yourself with your city, its various areas, and their locations. This way, when you encounter a specific address like 123 Main Street, you would already have some knowledge about the area, your potential buyers, and their preferences. For instance, you would know the criteria your buyers are looking for, such as their price range and closing period.

When dealing with potential buyers, it's important to know their preferences. You should ask them about the number of bedrooms and bathrooms they require, whether they want a corner lot, and whether they prefer a property in B, C, or A condition. Understanding your buyers' criteria is key to finding them the right property. Once you have identified your buyers' preferences, you can match them to the right property. For instance, if you have three buyers interested in 123 Main Street, you can quickly determine whether the property meets their specific needs. So, that's when everything will start coming together. Once you make connections, you'll realize that you're onto something. It's okay to have a casual conversation with the buyer and say, "Hey, I found something in this area that costs around this much. Are you still interested?" This is when you put out feelers and create hype. This is where the actual work begins.

You want to gain trust and get their approval in writing. When you're talking to the seller, you want to do a letter of intent and let them know you want to send it to their lawyer so they can review it before they sign it. This will build a lot of trust with them because they see you are doing everything ethically and legally and are doing things the right way.

You will send this to their lawyers for review. They will confirm what is not yet signed, sealed, and delivered. But it is enough that you have informed them of our intentions. We need to make sure that their lawyers approve of this deal as many deals fall apart in their office. For instance, if you offer $100,000 for a property, the lawyer may see the letter of intent and decide to reject the deal.

The reality of it is, the reason we sent it to a lawyer is that we want to show them we're coming in good faith. If the lawyer is going to kill the deal, the lawyer can kill the deal today or they can kill the deal in 30 days from now when you're ready to close it. The lawyer might as well just get that out of the way now and then it didn't cost you anything but a bit of your time. Then proceed, assuming the lawyer's consent, review, sign, and return it.

What to Say to a Motivated Seller

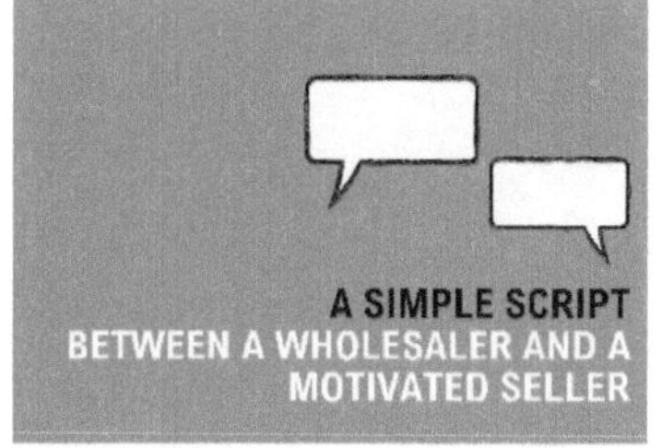

https://app.bitly.com/Bo4pjwghIeQ/http://bit.ly/3WYDxqX

Chapter 4

Now you know that they're in the game since they've signed a letter of intent. You know they have the intention that you've negotiated a price and a closing date. We have some idea that there's a possibility of a deal here. They're serious about moving forward. I cannot stress enough, if you're seeing the property in person or meeting the seller in person, ask if you can take pictures and videos. I highly recommend 50-100 pictures. When you are talking to a seller, you may hear their kids playing in the background, or their spouse may be around. They might also be unhappy or disgruntled, which can make the conversation uncomfortable. They could be walking around and staring at you, which can also add to the discomfort.

This makes it hard to notice everything when you walk into the property. I always walk in asking permission to take pictures and videos first. You can leave it to their discretion about videos, but pictures are a must. We have to have pictures. If you're doing this remotely and you won't be seeing the property yourself and you won't be sending anyone over there to take pictures, if you're relying on the seller, I strongly suggest you tell them how important it is to see all the good points of the property. For example, show me that new roof that you just put in, the bathroom just renovated, and the new electrical work you did. Let them know I also need to see the things that you think might need to be repaired in the next five years.

There is strategy behind the five-year mark. Instead of alarming them by listing all the immediate repairs, it's better to present them with a plan. If we only tell them what needs to be done right away, they might get scared and avoid it altogether. And in fact, frankly, sellers are so used to sometimes living in that condition that they don't see the problem anymore. We purchased a property from a wholesaler, and when we met the seller to finalize everything, we found out that the house was in a terrible condition. There was no running toilet or water in the sink, the heat was just wood, and there was no furnace. To make things worse, the house was a hoarder's house, and it was impossible to walk within two feet of anything. On top of that, the sewer wasn't working, and the whole place needed to be overhauled.

If no one would have been home, I really thought it was an abandoned property. There are two things here. One is that we're doing a service, we're helping people live in better conditions and the other part is that when you're going to wholesale it to an investor or an investor buyer, if they're going to be living in it, you want them to know the full picture, you want them to know everything about this property. You can now send pictures and videos of the property without the inspector and investor being physically present. This approach is less invasive for the seller, as they can simply view the media files instead of having someone on their property.

If the property pictures are good, detailed and clear, then I'm going to decide. Do I want to take on something that needs that much repair and if I am looking for something like that I may come out and say, "Well, Mr. wholesaler Miss wholesaler, you have said that it's approximately $50,000 to repair this property up to its condition. I'm estimating by your pictures it's $100,000." The status of the foundation is huge. I had issues with foundation in the past, both with new builds and old properties. In one case, I didn't even realize the house wasn't attached to the foundation.

One property I encountered had a foundation that was bowing inwards. Another property had a compromised main support beam. The beam had been cut, perhaps because it was deemed to be in the way. As a result, the house started to cave and crack. It's important to inspect the foundation for any cracks, whether it's supported by pillars, posts, cement blocks, or a stone foundation (which typically indicates age). This doesn't mean it's a major issue, but it's crucial to be transparent with potential buyers. If they express interest in the property and want to see it, show them everything, not just the good parts.

If they show up and they see a problem, and you didn't disclose it to them, they will not trust you. You've just burned a bridge with a buyer. I once went to look at a property from a wholesaler and when I showed up that day, the basement had three inches of water, and it smelled like sewer. Right away, I called the wholesaler to tell them they didn't disclose this to me, and I got out of the deal. I drove a distance to reach the property and even rented a car instead of using my vehicle. This shows how important it was to me.

As you're walking around a property, notice the corners of the ceilings and look straight up to see if the roof is leaking, especially in the upstairs part. Look at the floor. Is it in unison? Does it go from ceramic tile to hardwood, to plank, to parkade, to vinyl laminate, to nothing, to carpet? Considering the fact that an investor will examine the flooring and think about the cost of replacing it. They might consider ripping out everything and installing a new carpet or laminate flooring if necessary. These are important factors to consider.

An investor is going to be looking for damage such as holes in the wall, damage around the windows, broken windows, or missing doorknobs. If the walls have holes, nails, or wallpaper, it is considered damage even if the rooms are painted in different colors. An investor who's looking at fixing and flipping this property is going to consider that the wallpaper needs to be taken down and everything repainted. When considering this investment, they are mindful of making everything stage-proof and bringing it to A-plus moving condition.

I really want you to keep your eyes open when you walk in. It is going to be hard to notice everything and remember everything. That is why your pictures will help you afterwards. I often use my phone camera while inspecting a property for any issues. It helps me to quickly take pictures of everything without making a big deal about any problems I come across. This way, I can easily capture any mold growing or any other issues and keep a record of everything. I maintain a consistent and neutral tone throughout the inspection, and don't point out any problems with the seller. I just smile and keep going. In case the seller leaves some items behind, I don't have any issues with that, as long as they are not personal belongings.

To put it simply, it's important to empathize with the other person and make them feel understood. They need to know that you are on their side and that you are not insulting them. It's important to remember that while we may view a situation as a transaction or a matter of property, they may see it differently. So, it's crucial to be sensitive to their perspective and feelings to maintain a positive relationship.

If one of the kitchen cabinets has either a broken handle or a broken door and you can't replace that door and you may have to replace all the kitchen cabinets so that it matches. That can get costly. Are there any missing appliances, such as a dishwasher? Are the fridge and stove included? Are they in working condition? It is important that we disclose everything, and we bring it to an investor's attention. When you walk into bathrooms, mold is huge. That's probably the biggest thing. I remember one time we had to redo a bathroom and take down the ceiling, and to our surprise, there were carcasses of squirrels that fell out. I'm not kidding. Fixing a bathroom can be a major repair. When you look closer, check if the tub is scratched, leaking around the perimeter, or if there are any other issues. Sometimes, parents with children may face problems where all the water from the shower ends up on the other side of the tub, causing mold to grow along the tub's side. Eventually, the floor may get damaged as well.

Check to see if the toilets are leaking all the time because the water bill can be unbelievable. It will be one of the first things that you'd want to fix as an investor. When you're experiencing issues with your plumbing system, there are some things that you can check. For instance, if the toilet doesn't flush properly or if there is low water pressure when you flush it, you may have a plumbing problem. You can also check if the floor around the toilet is soft, which may indicate a more severe issue that requires fixing. In such cases, you may need to remove the toilet, vanity, and redo the floor. Another sign of plumbing issues is when running the tap in the sink and the tub simultaneously.

You will want to be aware of mold. Mold can be in the shower. Determine if the room has an exhaust fan. The presence of a window is also a factor to consider. In most cities, it is required by code that if there is a window, an exhaust fan is unnecessary. Conversely, if there is no window, an exhaust fan is required. I've been to some properties where there were no exhaust fan and no window. That's a problem. If there is no ventilation, mold will be created. You want to walk into a property and act like you are going to buy this place. Please note that for any heating or air conditioning system, there should be a tag or imprints of model numbers. Without these tags, the system will not pass an inspection, so it's crucial to ensure they are present. When dealing with a wood-burning fireplace, make sure that you obtain a special certificate to ensure that it's safe. Inhaling fumes from an unsafe fireplace can be fatal, so it's essential to be very careful. If you have a central air conditioning system, you can also use the model number to determine how old it is. By checking the model number and asking your HVAC contractor, you can find out what year it was made and if it's still in good condition.

If the property has a central air system, it's important to look for any tags, imprints of model numbers, or other identifying information. This will allow you to ask contractors about the age of the system and its lifespan. For example, a furnace typically lasts 7 to 10 years, while a boiler lasts up to 30 to 50 years. Having this information will help you determine if any appliances need to be replaced. When discussing the property with a potential buyer, it's useful to confidently refer to the tags and information you've gathered, as well as any insights from contractors.

In the bedrooms, lift the carpets. I can't tell you how many times that I've seen rugs covering holes, covering problems, covering pieces missing in the flooring. This will be an extra expense to deal with. One thing that I have done in a carpeted bedroom is to remove the floor grate. This allows the heat to come in directly from the floor. Now that I have removed all the carpet, I have discovered a beautiful hardwood floor underneath, which did not cost me anything extra. All I had to do was remove the carpet. This is a helpful trick for anyone looking to improve their flooring.

With bedrooms, it's important to have at least one window in each room. This is especially true if the room is a good size. Otherwise, if that's not there, it's not considered a bedroom. They might say to you, yes, it's a four-bedroom house, but if two of the bedrooms don't have any windows, then they're not considered bedrooms, it's considered a den. Again, that affects your property value and affects your after-repair value. This is because if an investor wants to buy the property, they have to make extensive renovations. Therefore, it is important to negotiate with this in mind and consider the potential costs of repairs when determining a fair price for the property.

The other thing about bedrooms is that they need closets. Check with the city for what the codes are. However, most times, if you don't have a closet, you can buy an armoire and get away with it. I can't tell you how many times I've looked inside closets, and I look up in the corner, and there's mold from the roof. Those are spots that people usually aren't paying attention to. They usually just have a bunch of stuff in their closets, so they're not really paying attention. Again, you want to take pictures, clear pictures and check the four corners of the closets. There isn't much on the floor of the closets, but it's important to be mindful of the baseboards around the perimeter. It can be tedious when you look at every little crack and an inspector is going to do that. I want to bring to your attention that we should keep an inspector's radar on the list of things we need to check. Even though we have them listed under a letter of intent, it's important to remember that all those items are part of a strategy we use. This strategy allows us to sell the property as is, as you want, and move by the date you specified. However, our investors are currently only able to come up with an unknown amount of X, considering our business model of buying these properties.

When a property is in an *as is* condition, it means that the owner wants to solve any problems with it, move on, and then restore the property to its full potential, bringing it back to an A-plus condition. Basements are an enormous investment. You need to check for water damage. Is it moldy down there? Does it smell down there?

Does it smell like a sewer down there? Is there a sump pump? Also look up at the walls in the basement. If the walls look like there's frosting on top of it, that's a problem. You're also going to want to check the foundation in the basement for cracks and whether the cracks are around the cement block or if they're in the middle of this cement block. Any cracks aren't good.

It is advisable to seek the assistance of a professional to assess any potential issues in the property you are dealing with. It is crucial to be cautious, especially in wholesaling, as the responsibility of the property eventually falls on the investor buyer. However, as a wholesaler, you should know any issues with the property and disclose them to the buyer. Some issues to check for include water damage, cracks in the foundation blocks, and holes in the foundation. It's important to give full disclosure of anything that you know about the property to avoid any future complications. I have noticed that sometimes, when wholesalers take pictures of electrical panels, they are missing important details. The panel may be blurry or foggy, making it difficult to read. It is crucial to take clear pictures, especially of the electrical panel. You should take close-up pictures to determine if it's a fuse or breaker panel. An inspector can also determine the amperage, although this is unnecessary for taking pictures.

When inspecting a house, it is important to examine the vanity, especially on the outside, as it may look good but have mold or water damage on the inside. The same goes for the kitchen sink and bathroom sink. Turn on the faucets, check if the tub, shower, and toilet are working properly. Sellers may not disclose all issues with the property as they want to sell for the highest price possible, so it's best to be cautious. Don't assume that they will tell you everything. Be mindful of any potential problems that may arise after purchasing the property.

When you're looking at the central air unit, you want to see how old it is. Take a picture. You also need to see the roof from the road. Go down a couple of blocks safely across the street, look both ways and take a picture of the roof from a different angle. That way you can get a better idea of it. Are there shingles missing? What kind of roof is it? Is it a steel roof or is it an asphalt shingle? Is there a bow on the roof? This will incur additional costs. Consider taking more pictures, even using Google Maps to take pictures at the addresses.

You will not get the same effect where a lot of times those pictures are old. It seems like you want to make sure you have proper eaves, troughs, face soffit, and siding on your property to keep it in good condition. These external elements may cost money, but they can prevent animals from getting in and water from seeping into your basement or crawlspace. Without eaves and troughs, water can erode over time and fall directly onto the foundation, leading to water damage inside the home. It's important to invest in these external features to avoid potential problems down the line.

Those are some things to be very mindful of. Consider the same thing with the garage as well. You always want to make sure on the outside that there's a slope away from your house because if there is bowing, the water is going to go directly into the basement. Build up dirt in a way that everything is cleaned. Some people may like to plant trees very close to their houses. However, I would suggest that such trees should be photographed and removed as soon as possible. This is because the roots of the trees can grow and cause significant damage to the house.

Similarly, some properties have vines growing on the outside, which can penetrate the foundation of the house through the mortar. Therefore, it is important to be aware of the potential risks associated with planting trees or vines near your house. If you're planning to sell your property, it's advisable to remove any mulch around the property, particularly around the foundation. Refrain from planting anything that requires frequent watering as it can cause damage to your property.

The property has some issues that need to be addressed. There are foundation blocks that may have cracks, holes in the walls, and a missing electrical panel. The eaves and troughs may be spacious, which is something to ask the seller about. Another important question to consider is whether all the equipment on the property is owned or rented. They may have recently installed a new furnace, central air system, or hot water tank, so it's important to clarify this with the seller. Suddenly, if they tell you that all the equipment is rented, it is important to make them understand that on the closing date, they will have to pay for it in full and you're not assuming any rental contract. This is a crucial point to remember.

When inspecting a garage, check for any signs of dilapidation. The city may require you to tear it down if it is in critical condition. In such cases, it is advisable to check with the city to see if it has been condemned. It is always best to be honest and upfront when dealing with such situations. Don't assume that you are being told the truth. Instead, ask questions and clarify any doubts you have.

When checking the garage, inspect the roof, walls, and foundation. Check if the garage is leaning or has any signs of water damage. It is also important to check if there is electricity going to the garage. By doing so, you can ensure that you are making an informed decision before investing in the property. Don't assume that they're telling you the truth, at least ask the questions.

In the garage also check the roof, and walls, is it leaning? Is there water in there? Is there electrical going to that garage? Is there a breaker panel of electricity that goes into that garage? Is there lighting? Is there heating? Are there a lot of windows? Are the windows in good condition? Are they broken? Is the garage door manual or powered? Is it functional? Is there stuff in the garage right now or in the shed? Will that be there on the closing date or are they going to be taking any of those items you want?

I just wanted to check if the garage has any issues. In the past, I've seen properties where backyard mechanics have worked and there were problems such as oil spills and gasoline in the garage. So, please be mindful of that when checking the garage.

If there's contamination, now suddenly you could be in for a very costly repair, depending on what level it is. Take a picture of the garage floor. See if there is oil, if there are oil spills, if there are gasoline spills. If there's an oil tank on the property, you want to know about that.

When looking to buy a property, it's important to ask a few questions to ensure you make the right investment. Firstly, ask if anyone has passed away on the property. It's also good to know how long the owners have owned the property and whether they have lived there themselves. If there are tenants, find out if they will vacate the property. Ask what the owners are taking with them when they move. Assure them they can leave anything behind if they wish to.

It's also important to note the condition of the neighboring properties. If the property you're interested in is the worst one on the block, that's a good sign. It means that the neighbors will appreciate any improvements you make to the property. If the property looks better than everything else in the neighborhood but has a lot of problems, it may affect the value of the property. Finally, note any eyesores in the neighborhood, such as junk cars or piles of garbage. This may not be a deal-breaker for an investor, but it's important to be aware of it.

Investors should be cautious when buying properties. They need to consider factors like the proximity of the property to neighbors or a nearby railroad track, which can cause noise and vibrations that affect the foundation of the building. The location of the property can show the income level of the area, such as whether neighbors park their cars in the garage or on the driveway. Investors should also check if the property is on a sidewalk that needs to be cleared of snow during winter. Being mindful of these factors will help investors make informed decisions and avoid unexpected expenses.

Another thing to make sure of is what is the yard like. Look at the landscaping. It is important to see whether there is good landscaping or the lack thereof. A dead tree in the back could cost $1000 to $3,000. Be mindful of these things as you're walking around the property.

When inspecting a property, it's important to check that all light fixtures are working properly and that the plumbing is functioning as well. You should also ensure that there is proper electrical wiring on the property. Another crucial aspect to check is the condition of the decks, especially if they are pressure-treated, as winter weather can cause damage and repairing them can be expensive. You'll want to make sure they are clear of any debris and that they are pressure-treated appropriately, as using the wrong treatment can lead to rot.

Overall, safety is key when inspecting a property, so it's important to be thorough and diligent in your inspection process. As you're going up the stairs, make sure that there are railings. Another thing is to install railings up to code on the outside. Is the property ready for someone with a disability? Also, notice if windows are needed on a property. It goes back to just taking a picture and you can determine later the count of the windows. Investors appreciate knowing the exact number of windows in a property because it helps them get accurate pricing information easily.

It is important to know how close a property is to water. How close is the property to a river or lake, and how close it is to the dock? How far is the property from the beach? Being aware of these details can help potential investors or buyers make informed decisions about the property. It is also important to know the location of big box stores like Home Depot, LCBO, and hardware stores in the area. This information can be useful for investors who plan to do renovations. Knowing that these stores are easily accessible can help them decide about the property.

It's important to be honest with potential buyers about the location of the property. If Home Depot is an hour away, let them know. You can suggest local hardware stores that may be smaller but have what they need. If they can't see the property in person, request lots of pictures. Good pictures are crucial for the investor partners. The better the pictures, the less likely they are to want to see the property multiple times. Sellers rarely want strangers in their home multiple times either. Encourage them to send as many pictures as possible. Over the phone, ask about any repairs needed in the next five years and note them as per the seller.

It's important to emphasize the significance of taking pictures and videos of a property and sharing them remotely. Sometimes, buyers purchase a property without seeing it in person, so it's crucial to have good enough pictures to understand what you're getting into. I have bought properties sight unseen many times because the wholesaler had provided me with satisfactory pictures. Knowing what's going on with the property is crucial, and I can't stress it enough.

Chapter 5

Chapter Five is about *how to do your due diligence*. It is about getting facts and numbers. Lesson 1 emphasizes the importance of beginning your due diligence by diving deep and investing time and energy in the process. While this may take some effort, it is a crucial step that cannot be overlooked. This is where people who don't have a coach lose a lot of money. A lot of investors I know and including myself, have lost money on the buy. What does this mean?

It's important to purchase the property at a lower price point, not just a discounted price, to attract investors along with investor buyers. There was one business venture that I went on and I lost $300,000. There was another one that I lost $30,000 because of foundation issues. There have been properties I've made that back. The biggest risk of not doing your due diligence when purchasing a property is that you may not be aware of what you don't know. For instance, a property may have been condemned in the past, which you can find out by checking with the city. It is crucial to know what the city has to say about the property before making a purchase.

What information can you gather about the property taxes and assessment? What has the realtor told you about the area? Have we discussed whether it's a buyer or a seller's market? What's the zoning and what are the city's plans for the next five years? To ensure that you conduct proper due diligence, you need to know as much as possible about the property and its surroundings within a mile or five-mile radius. What's going on with the property? Another way to make money on the buy is to buy a property and wholesale it to someone else. This happened to me when I could sell a property and still make $50,000. I conducted my due diligence and knew that the property's zoning would allow a severance. I could sell it to someone and hand over the possibility of severance by showing them an email from the city confirming that it was possible.

There are all kinds of opportunities. When considering a real estate investment, it's important to do your due diligence. One common mistake is valuing a property based solely on its location, such as being on a corner lot. While corner lots can be valuable, there may be other factors to consider. For example, instead of converting the property into two duplexes, you could renovate it and keep it as a single duplex. However, you need to be mindful of the costs involved. If you pay too much for the property or spend too much on repairs, you're likely to lose money. To be successful, aim to make your profit on the purchase, rather than relying on the value increasing after renovations. A good rule of thumb is to aim for a profit of at least $50,000 after all expenses are paid, such as repairs, carrying costs, marketing, and real estate agent fees.

Some investors are not concerned about the details of a deal. They may be attracted to a booming market, or simply unable to find properties. Sometimes, they may accept a smaller profit margin. However, I prefer to assign a specific value to the deal before proceeding. To get more details, Google the address and look under the news tabs. You can find out if there's been a crime in that area. If it is a high crime area, keep that in mind as some investors are specifically looking for properties in lower income areas, which is not necessarily a problem. However, the most important thing to consider when doing so is how you can tailor the property to fit the needs of your investor. In the beginning, I suggested you should first find your buyers. This way, when you come across a property that is in a less desirable area or is in poor condition, you can quickly sell it to your buyers. Such properties may be classified as a C location or may be in a C condition. It may be better to have the sellers list their properties otherwise, since we may not be able to help them.

The last thing that you want to do is put the property under contract and then not be able to sell it. To prove to others that you can solve their problem, it's important to show that you've done your due diligence. This means having potential buyers lined up, making a good offer, and personally inspecting the property or reviewing pictures. To solidify your numbers, consider hiring an inspector and appraiser to determine the property's as-is and after repair value. This will help you determine if it's worth spending money on the property.

Look for comparable locations that match square footage. I have received deals from wholesalers in the past that were not comparable, despite them claiming otherwise. For instance, they may offer a property for $325,000 and list comparables, but these comparables may be three to five miles away, which can make a vast difference. In some markets, a difference of a few miles can mean a significant change in value, especially in areas where million-dollar homes are only a mile away.

When you look at zoning, you want to compare apples to apples. When analyzing zoning, it's important to consider the specific use of the property. For example, if your property is zoned for single family use, you'll want to compare it to other properties with the same zoning. Comparing it to properties with different zoning, such as commercial or duplex, would not provide accurate comparisons. It's important to make sure you're comparing apples to apples to get an accurate understanding of the property's value. When you renovate and convert a property, its value increases. This is an important consideration for investors who are interested in buying. As a buyer, do your due diligence and look for comparable properties. This will help you sell your contract more successfully. For instance, if your subject property has one bathroom, compare it to other properties with one bathroom. Similarly, if your property has two bedrooms, compare it to other properties with two bedrooms. It's important to note that this information should not be disclosed to the seller.

When considering building an additional unit in the basement of a property, it is important to check with the city to confirm what the code is for basement height. This is crucial because if the height of your basement is too low, say only five feet, you may not be able to construct an additional unit because of code restrictions. As far as making it extra living space, you don't want to compare that to something that has seven feet basement height because that would give it a different value. You could overpay for that property, the condition of the property, as is an ARV.

Evaluate what the property needs. How is the roof? Then, it's important to look at the comparables and see how the properties in the area have sold - whether they were sold as is or if everything in the area was done up nicely. It's also important to note what they were sold for at that point, because this helps establish what the property will be worth when the investor is done fixing it up. With this information, you can create a buyer's package that includes these comps.

You can't compare a 30 by 50 lot with a 300 by 500 lot. Lot size can determine again if you can build another garage or a shed or if you can build another property on there. When comparing properties, the lot size is a critical factor. It's important to have accurate information on the lot size to determine if the price aligns with the spread and if it's a good investment opportunity for buyers.

I would like to suggest a strategy where I offer to buy a property at a price that is 25% or lower than its estimated worth. For instance, if a property is worth around $400,000, I will offer to buy it for under $300,000. This way, I can secure a good deal at a lower price and can sell it to an investor buyer. I prefer this approach rather than committing to a higher price and then having to renegotiate with the seller later. It is better to walk away from a deal before agreeing to it and wasting everyone's time.

It is possible to get a bonus if you have a corner lot with the potential to sever the land, change the zoning and add a dwelling unit. Having a corner lot means you can subdivide it into two lots, which would give you two frontages. You can then sell one lot and get the other one for free. Investors find this opportunity attractive, although it's important to note that getting a land severance takes time and is not guaranteed. However, you could still mention the possibility of it in your listing. To confirm the chance of a land severance, you can contact the city and ask if it's possible. If the city confirms this in an email, it's a good sign. We always appreciate seeing such opportunities.

Are you wondering if it's possible to change the zoning of a property to allow for more units? Whether it's changing from commercial to mixed-use residential or creating a duplex or mother-in-law suite, you'll need to contact the city to find out if it's possible. They can advise you on if the property has enough entrances and exits to accommodate additional units.

Take those items into consideration again. You want to be mindful of corner lots and zoning when you walk through properties. I strongly suggest that you go through a lot of properties and a lot of open houses. I literally engulf myself by going to look at real estate all the time. I've seen hundreds of houses. By seeing that many properties, you start to compare and evaluate numerous properties, and eventually close on one, you need to understand the possibilities. With the right knowledge, you can walk into a property and assess its potential for improvement. For instance, you can easily identify if you can add another bedroom by examining the location of the windows. This can increase the property's value and generate more profit for you as an investor. The more you learn, the more you can share with potential investors, and the more money you can make.

They will keep returning to you to check the comparisons for potential future value if taken to its highest and best use, which can be a game-changing strategy. So, when you're conversing with the city officials and inquiring about the best possible use for a particular area or property that you are interested in acquiring, the city will be honest with you about their interest in that property. This can be an incredible lesson. To get some assistance with your due diligence, you can contact a local realtor and ask them about the neighborhood.

Previously I discussed how to contact realtors and what to say to them. You have a general idea about the city and what's happening there. Now, what we need to do is to focus on it more specifically. I cannot disclose the address right now because I don't have a non-disclosure agreement or a non-circumventing agreement in place. These agreements are necessary to protect my interests, and it is like guarding my food dish. As I have this property under contract, I am cautious about sharing the information because realtors are mainly interested in selling properties, and I want to be careful about it. Therefore, I make sure that I have the property under a secure contract before giving out any information.

I attempted to ask them if there was anything I needed to be aware of in the vicinity. Perhaps they had spoken to someone before about the city, which is large, and now they could provide me with more specific information. For example, what's it like near the corner store? What's it like near the school? What's it like near the park? What's it like near the hardware store? I suggested they speak to a top producer who primarily deals with investors and let them know that I may have a deal coming up, and I will sell my assignable contract.

It's helpful to inform realtors you are a wholesaler who assigns contracts, so that they can connect you with buyers. You can explain that motivated sellers reach out to you, and you get deals under contract. Adding the commission on top of the wholesale fee is not a problem for you. It's important to work with a realtor who supports wholesalers and understands how they operate. This can make the process smoother and more profitable for everyone involved. By being transparent and disclosing your intentions, you can protect yourself and avoid any misunderstandings. More and more realtors realize the benefits of working with wholesalers.

If you are selling something to someone who is unsure about it, it's important to be honest with them about what you do. If they have a different opinion, you can always look for another realtor to work with. Being self-employed means you have the freedom to choose who you work with. If you want to protect yourself from losing potential sales, ask your lawyer to create a non-disclosure non-circumventing agreement. This way, once they sign it, they won't be able to circumvent your agreement and make the sale on their own. This is not in their best interest, so it's a good idea to have a signed agreement in place.

Lesson three is about deciding whether the numbers work. Proceed to the next step only if the numbers can work. If the numbers don't work, approach the seller and inform them that the investor has only a specific amount of cash to do the deal. Here's a strategy that I use: I do of due diligence and figure out what needs to be done. Then I approach the situation with a plan in mind, knowing what needs to be done.

My buyer is still going to be interested. I want to make sure that it's going to be a deal to my buyer. I've negotiated $150,000. In the past, I have said to the seller right now my investor has $110,000 to invest in this property. I don't say that I'm making an offer of $110,000. I just tell them that is all they have. They argue their rebuttal is necessary to close the deal.

If you're feeling hesitant and think that it requires too much effort, then it might be better to politely decline. Let the person know that if they change their mind, they can always contact you. This happens often. If they lower it to that amount, which makes the numbers work so far, then redo the letter of intent and send it to them. They signed it, so all you have to do is adjust the price, put a line through the old price, initial it, and send it back to them. Alternatively, you can meet with them and sign it so that we can move forward.

We really need to manage our emotions since it can be such an emotional roller coaster. Sellers are beautiful people, and they are just scared. They want the most because this is their biggest asset. They know that this was the biggest decision in their lives, so they're going to guard it. Even though they can't afford that property, even though they can't afford to keep up that property, it doesn't matter. They're still going to get the most out of it. You need to know that not every deal is a deal and not every lead is a deal. Be mindful that not every seller will work out.

Chapter 6

We have to appear content and confident and actively prepare to attain victory. We must make sure that we are fully prepared to write up the offer and move from the Letter of Intent to a binding contract.

When making an offer, it's important to send all the details of the terms negotiated with the seller to your attorney. This ensures that everything is done legally, ethically, and morally, and that your interests are covered. You want to make sure that you are protected from any potential legal action that may arise because of any actions you take or fail to take. The terms should include the negotiated closing date, and any other important details related to the purchase agreement.

It's important to ensure that you follow the law when making property deals. Remember that just because you receive an offer from your lawyer or attorney, it doesn't mean that you can use it on multiple properties. It's not recommended to write up your own offers, since every city has different laws and regulations that change frequently. Some cities may not allow wholesaling, so it's crucial to ensure that you know the laws and have everything done legally.

When setting the terms and conditions of the deal, consider the closing date and purchase price. It's recommended to include a $100 deposit in the agreement. Specify the contingencies such as an inspection, appraisal, or multiple contractor visits. You can also negotiate with the seller to keep the property in good condition or allow for vacant possession. It's important to clarify the terms of the deal to avoid any misunderstandings later.

When entering into a contract for a property, it is crucial to ensure that the contract clearly states whether there is a tenant currently occupying the property, and if so, whether they will be vacating. Seeking advice from a lawyer or attorney is recommended to ensure that the contract is worded correctly. As a wholesaler looking to assign the contract to an investor buyer, it is important to inform the lawyer of your intention and seek their advice on conditions and contingencies. You should also ensure that there is enough time for the investor to conduct their due diligence. Even though you have already done your own research, the investor will probably want to do the same, and any third-party information you have can help streamline the process.

If you have received an email from the city after visiting there, you can forward it to your investor buyer. If you have comparables that closely match the information discussed previously, it would be helpful to send those to your buyer as well. It is important to include as many details as possible when communicating important information to your lawyer or attorney. Their primary role is to protect you, and having all the information will help them do their job effectively. Once an offer is assigned to an investor buyer, you want to ensure that you are no longer responsible for closing the transaction.

It's important to ensure that others understand what you're doing, so be clear with them about your intentions and the conditions that must be met for approval. Consult with your lawyer or attorney to make sure you haven't overlooked any important details. Ask for their input on the conditions and any contingencies that may arise. They may suggest a time frame for these conditions, such as 14 days, 7 days, or 30 days. It's important to follow their advice because they are licensed and insured and can help prevent errors and omissions.

One suggestion that you made was to include a clause acknowledging that your lawyer has approved the offer, which you are already getting since your lawyer is handling the deal. If I'm dealing one with a real estate agent, I would include a similar clause that requires your attorney's approval before finalizing the deal. This would ensure that you have legal protection, and that the property seller would allow access to the property up to three times for contractors, appraisers, inspectors, and investor partners. You already are taking some precautions by collecting pictures of the property as part of your business model.

Now, what you want is to have people come and view the property in person. You can make it mandatory for them to come in up to three times to ensure they are serious and won't back out. To ensure that you are protected, it is important to have access to the property to carry out necessary tasks. It is advisable to inform the seller that you will be present when they come in or access the property. This helps in maintaining a good relationship with the seller and avoids any unwanted surprises. It is important to keep the seller informed and be available to answer their queries. If someone else is sent in your place, it may create confusion and disrupt the deal. Therefore, it is essential to keep the seller close and maintain a good relationship with them.

A lot of times the sellers really feel better only dealing with you. If you have been working remotely with the team through phone and suddenly you decide to send someone to the property, it is possible to do so as long as you give explicit instructions to that person. Make sure they understand their role is limited to showing a contractor around, getting quotes, letting an appraiser in, or assisting an inspector. It's important to have clear communication to avoid any confusion or misunderstandings.

When an investor partner is meeting with the seller and you are not present, the conversation might involve language that you are not familiar with. However, investors usually have a good understanding of the language used. It is important that you go into the meeting as one of our investor partners and ask any questions you may have. Please direct your questions to me instead of to the seller. This way, the seller will only provide information and not negotiate with you directly. As long as you're doing everything ethical, and the seller knows what's going on, everybody knows what's going on, then everybody plays nice, because the seller wants to sell, and the buyer wants to buy and all you're doing is facilitating it. It is really important to be transparent, honest, and ethical.

They must allow you to market their property to cash buyers and their contacts. So, in some of my offers, I have included a clause stating that the seller agrees to my terms. It's about being transparent and making sure they know what you do. I work in wholesale and specialize in bringing together buyers and sellers. I excel in problem-solving and strive to ensure that the process is seamless for my clients. I don't charge any commissions and aim to keep everything transparent so that my clients have no surprises. They are usually more comfortable knowing what's happening every step of the way. It's always best to avoid situations where someone may come up to them and say that they have seen their property listed on Facebook without their knowledge. I believe in being transparent with certain deals. By informing the other party of my plans, such as marketing the property, it helps build trust. After all, even a realtor's job is to market the property they are selling. However, in my case, I am marketing my contract and not the actual property. This approach helps to clarify that I am selling the contract, not the property itself.

Let the seller know you are part of a group of investors who can make a cash offer based on one appraisal and a home inspection, and that you would like to see the property at no cost. Explain to the seller what it was like when they bought their house. If they remember, they were probably not given a lot of detail. When my students are doing a wholesale deal with a seller, they tell them a lot more. They're giving them a lot more information. They're talking to them more. They will not remember 90% of what you say, but the biggest thing is that if you say it, you can always revert to it and let them know we covered it.

You can let them know we can cover it again. This gives credibility versus them coming back to you and saying something was not disclosed. They only want an appraisal and a home inspection and to see the property. They just want a quick and easy solution. It doesn't matter if the property is in good condition or not. I have already taken pictures and gone through the details with them. Sometimes, I ask them what their preferences are, but mostly I make the process as simple as possible. I don't want to add any more stress to their already difficult situation. People who are motivated to sell are usually in a hurry and have some financial constraints. They need to sell their property fast, and that's why they are reaching out to us. I try to be patient and understanding with them.

It is important for you to manage your emotions, especially when they are overwhelming and causing chaos in your mind. It's like your emotions are tap dancing and exploding all at once. It's crucial to have someone you can rely on like a life preserver, and that's why every seller gravitates towards me. I stay in contact with them. I reach out to them by text, email, or phone call almost every day through this entire process because I just want to let them know I'm here. This is going on in the background to let them know there is a lot of reassurance. There is a lot of babysitting, but it is worth it at the end of the day

There's a lot of money we've made in real estate, and there's a lot of people that need to be helped. A lot of times a seller just needs to get themselves out of their own way. If someone sells their property in a panic, it's usually because they didn't take care of the problem earlier. If they had addressed the issue, they could have sold the property at market value, invested in the repairs, or avoided having to sell altogether. It's important to remember that there were likely a series of decisions or life changes that led to the situation, rather than a sudden irrational decision.

Chapter 7

It's important to be prepared for the three viewings in Chapter 7. Firstly, schedule a meet and greet with the potential buyers. Set up three dates and times for the appraiser, inspector, and investor to view the property. It's essential to ask them about their availability and preferences. Inquire about their preferred time of day - morning, afternoon, or evening, and whether they're available during the week or on weekends. This will make the process more convenient for everyone involved.

It is important to accommodate without delaying the deal. Have a conversation with them and stress the importance of these meetings so that you can move forward. There are going to be contractors coming in, so it's important to let them know that you only require quotes. This is all part of the process that will take place.

The appraiser and inspector will view the property together on the first date. It is crucial that you are present at the property to coordinate everything, as so many things can go wrong if you are not there. There can be conversations among the appraiser, inspector, and homeowner, and they may say things that an investor should not hear. It happens often, and a lot of issues can arise during a wholesale deal. Therefore, it is essential that you are there to prevent any potential problems.

I also know that a lot of things can go right. A lot of it is - are you able to be there? I know a lot of wholesalers that would rather do things remotely. I've done them remotely as well. However, I want to point out that there are various challenges that come with scheduling second and third dates, booking investors and contractors, and ensuring that the appraisal and inspection are completed. It's important to have someone you trust present during these processes.

On the second or third date, after I have done some initial research, run some numbers, and have a pretty good idea of what's going on, I like to schedule an appraisal if I've already analyzed the situation and found a good deal. Once I have done the comps and run all the numbers, it's worth me putting money out to get an actual as-is appraisal and an after-repair-value appraisal.

It is important and worth it to get something in writing to let the investor buyer know you have disclosed everything. There may be a potential scenario where you offer your knowledge to a buyer, but there may be some dispute over your fees. However, as long as the buyer can make a profit from what they're purchasing, they should be satisfied with the transaction. You mentioned a wholesaler who specializes in after repair value appraisals and doesn't conduct inspections.

There's a lot to be said about some wholesalers who are doing inspections and appraisals. One way to attract an investor without a physical meeting is to have a remote investor who has local contractors and a well-established business. If you can get free inspections online and send them via email, they will see it as an asset. Experienced investors who are your potential clients would also know the cost of things.

To ensure success, hire somebody in the local marketplace that can be a right-hand person you can trust to meet the appraiser, the inspector and even investors when they come out. Having boots on the ground is just good business. When you cannot make it out, it is important to have this right-hand person you trust meet with the investors in your place, since it builds confidence and trust.

For example, when a wholesaler refers me to the seller when I want to view the property, it's awkward. It's awkward because the seller is expecting to see the wholesaler they have been working with and have built a relationship with and when that wholesaler is not there, it makes it awkward to discuss why they are not there.

Chapter 8

Chapter 8 will discuss contractors. It is getting fun now because you are getting renovation quotes. It is fun but challenging because some contractors don't want to come out and see the property.

I can instead call them with an inspection in hand and ask what the cost would be to fix these five items on the inspection. Chances are they will give you a ballpark range in cost. Now you've saved their time, gas, and energy. They know their prices off the top of their head. So, now they can give you an estimate and you can say, "I need something in writing. I'm going to be selling this property and to know how much it's going to cost to fix it up." That's how I would address it with the contractor. I'm buying this property, and I need an idea of what it's going to cost to renovate it. Now, you can pass that estimate on to the investor buyer.

You can pass that on to the investor, letting them know I have quotes based on the inspection to fix these five higher ticket items. By giving them the estimate, you're providing the investor buyer with a hassle-free package. You're putting in a lot of effort to make sure everything is taken care of, and you've earned your profit on the property by doing so. By handing it over to them, they appreciate the convenience and benefit from it.

Chapter 9

Chapter 9 is about communicating with your buyers. If you have received the appraisal, inspection report, and contractor quotes, you have a couple of days left to showcase the property as per the contingency clause in your offer's conditions. You still have two appointments left you can utilize. Therefore, it's the best time to reach out to your buyers' list and market the property so that more people can have a look at it.

Lesson 1 is about preparing a package for the buyer. You should include pictures, videos, description, zoning, and comparables. You should also find the ARV appraisal value, but I wouldn't include the report in the package. Just let them know that you have it and tell them that the inspection is available to them. If they're serious, include cost estimates you got from the contractors, things that you noted about the condition, and suggestions on the repairs needed for maximum profit. When looking at the buyer's package, keep it brief and present the information with bullet points.

I have some tips when presenting a property to potential buyers. It's important to include pictures, zoning information, and any other details you notice. When communicating with them, it's best to have confidence in what you're saying, and one way to do that is by walking the property yourself. This is especially important in the investor world, where asking a wholesaler if they've walked the property can reveal a lot about the potential deal. I often ask wholesalers if they would buy the property themselves, as I can quickly analyze the deal and determine if it's worthwhile.

I've turned it on them and said, would you buy this? They've looked at me and said no. I pause, and I sit back and tell them, "I want to impress upon you if it's not a deal that excites you and you would not buy this home yourself, I strongly suggest you let the deal go." How can you sell something if you don't believe in it?

I worked as a mortgage broker for almost 15 years. Whenever I had to connect investors with lenders, they would come to me for deals. Especially, if we had to seek hard money lenders or private money, my lenders would ask me, 'Theresa, would you do this deal? At first, I considered one or two, but then I turned down a lot of business because they didn't seem profitable. However, for the rest of them, I could confidently show the lenders why I would do the deal and even explain my reasoning. If they asked me why I would do it, I was always prepared to give a solid answer. However, if they turned it around and asked me why I wouldn't do it, I had to admit that I wasn't in the financial position to take the risk.

Have the outlook that you believe in this product and ask yourself if you would sell this to your mother. We call it the Mom Test. Ask yourself if you would sell this property to your mother. If your answer is yes, then you're on the right track. Sometimes, when suggesting renovations that yield maximum profit, we overcomplicate things. To determine the after-repair value, we consult an appraiser and base the value on the five most expensive items that need fixing-foundation, roof, HVAC, plumbing, and electrical. If these items are upgraded or replaced, we can estimate the after-repair value. This information can then be used when speaking to investors or buyers, informing them of the cost of fixing these five things and the estimated value of the property after repair.

Presenting the suggested renovations to the investor, third-party documentation from licensed professionals, can yield a max profit. Comparables are a useful tool for real estate investors. They provide information about recently sold properties in the area, which can help investors determine the potential value of a property they are interested in. The great thing about comparables is that they are objective and based on third-party documentation from licensed professionals. Investors don't have to rely on the opinions of others-they can simply look at the data and make their own decisions. All a wholesaler needs to do is provide the link to the property and the price of the contract, including the wholesale fee.

When you're selling a contract of a property, it's important to provide documentation that supports your claims. You want to make sure that you include third-party information to back up what you're saying. This will help ease any doubts or concerns that potential investors may have. As much as investors want to buy a property, they're also looking for a reason not to buy it. It's important to provide as much evidence as possible to convince them it's a great deal.

When investors hear this is a great deal, they are scared that the wholesalers will not be honest with them and disclose everything. Therefore, the investors will try to find problems with it.

It's important to prepare a buyer's package that is concise and easy to understand. You want to make sure it packs a punch and provides enough information to pique their interest. However, avoid overwhelming them with too much information. It's also important to include the non-disclosure and non-circumventing agreements to prevent them from going behind your back and making a deal with the property owner. You can provide these documents, excluding the address, and give them an idea of the location of the property.

I have an example of a buyer's package that I typically send out. The package includes a one-page email containing an exclusive investment opportunity, property overview, and address (if you feel comfortable sharing it). You can also choose to include the vicinity or city if you prefer. It includes information on the number of bedrooms and bathrooms, whether there's a full basement, and any other features that the property may have. If it's a double lot, that would also be noted.

When creating a buyer's list, wholesalers often focus on one specific city. If this is the case, you can send out a non-disclosure non-circumventing agreement to all buyers on your list ahead of time. This ensures that they've already signed it before being presented with the property information. Then, when you send out the buyer's package, you can include the address and city of the property. This is another way to go about it.

The basement is already full, but when you mention the potential for additional features like an ADU or a double lot, they imagine the possibilities. They now know that there's potential for an additional dwelling unit and more money to be made. They can even make it a two-unit double lot. An investor might think, *Wait a minute, I can sever the condition, do a full rehab as needed.* It's important to be upfront about the condition of the property. If it needs a lot of work, it's easier to say *full rehab* rather than listing out every individual thing that needs to be done.

For the property's possession, buyers are curious whether there will be a tenant on the closing date. They want to know if they can start working on the property right away after the closing day. This information is crucial to them. The investment highlights of the property include its Class-A location, and if it's not a Class-A location, it may be classified as Class B.

If you're dealing with a Class B location, you'll need to adjust the way you describe it. Highlight its strategic location, proximity to schools, waterfront, grocery stores, and hardware stores for a convenient and attractive lifestyle. Don't forget to mention the location's proximity to a big city, which could be a highlight. You can say, "Less than 20 minutes away from [Big City]" to emphasize the potential for urban connectivity and rental demand. Keep in mind that some properties might be located outside of a big city, so it's important to highlight their proximity to one.

An investor may let you know they do not want to live on the property, they want to BRRRR, which is to buy repair, rent, refinance and repeat. They want to generate this property as rental income. In that case, you can suggest an alternative approach by presenting them with the information about a high-value property that was recently sold nearby for over $500,000. This information shows a strong potential for equity growth and could provide them with another option to consider.

If you have already analyzed the surrounding market, the numbers and facts you present are not made up, but a summary of what you know about the property. By simplifying and organizing this information, you can provide a quick and clear overview to potential investors, enabling them to decide if they are interested in contacting you.

Your goal is to reach as many people as possible and present them with high-quality equity growth comprehensive reports. All you need to mention is that the ARV appraisal is available and supports the projected $500,000 ARV. By doing so, you can show them that nearby properties are selling for the same amount. You can provide them with the inspection report, which offers transparency regarding the property's current conditions. As an investor, when you see *full rehab needed,* it could mean anything from the house being about to fall down to just needing some fresh paint, cleaning, a few bathrooms, and a new kitchen.

A full rehab means different things to different people. When an investor sees full rehab, they usually think the worst. It's challenging to determine the property's current condition and be transparent about it, as everyone views things differently. An inspection report from a third party can help in this situation. For instance, while you may think the property requires a full rehab, the inspection report may indicate that it needs to be torn down or that it just needs cosmetic changes. Although it is difficult to satisfy everyone, a third-party report can provide a clear picture of the property's condition.

I took a picture of the house and uploaded it. The picture shows the front of the house, including its color, door, shrubs, and any sign in the front. I marketed my assignable contract for $325,000, including the wholesale fee. I informed them that the closing date was set for June 1st of the current year. By doing so, I have given them a clear idea of how much money they need and when they need to make the purchase.

Investment strategies are important to consider when looking to invest in property. There are three key strategies I would recommend. Firstly, the property fix and flips exit strategy. This involves purchasing a property, making necessary repairs, and then selling it for a profit.

Secondly, the BRRRR strategy. This strategy involves buying a property, rehabbing it, renting it out, refinancing it, and then having a tenant in place. This is a great long-term strategy for investors.

Lastly, the wholesale strategy is a quick way to make money. This involves selling the assignable contract for the property to another investor as is, after buying it at a lower price. Wholesaling can be a profitable strategy for investors. Sometimes, they don't even have to do anything about it.

You might have left such a gap between the $325,000 and the $500,000. They suddenly realize they could sell it to someone else for a higher price, making a profit. That helps because they have to close it. If they have their own cash to put in the deal or they have access to hard money lenders or a joint venture partner, those are opportunities where wholesale can really come into play. If you need to quickly close a deal and you're taking a minimal wholesale fee, then you can offer your buyers a bulk of the profit. However, the challenge is that you need to close this deal within a week.

Due to a lack of time, many wholesalers get greedy and jeopardize deals by refusing to negotiate fees or lower prices. Instead, they would rather lose the deal and ruin credibility with the seller, which makes no sense. It's better to negotiate and bring the price down to facilitate and successfully close the deal. This way, everyone involved benefits, and the wholesaler's reputation remains unharmed.

Contractor quotes are available because, again, you've already covered that, that you've got those so you can send those out to them as well. Financing options are available. We previously discussed how you'd be sitting down with a branch manager to find out if it's a buyer's market or a seller's market or if people are losing their properties. As you progress through the chapters, learn to talk to people and complete your assignments, as you will gain valuable knowledge. When you are speaking to a buyer, for instance, you can mention your experience visiting a bank and the services they offer. You can even provide the name and contact information of the person you spoke to, so the buyer can reach out to them directly. This way, you can help the investor buyer make informed decisions and solve their problems more efficiently.

Now you can offer a joint venture option to others. You can tell them you have already done your homework on the property and are convinced that it will generate profits. You can offer to take care of the renovations, contractors, budget, and all the details while they buy the property. Later, when they sell the property, you can split the profits. This is a great option for people who have money but no time or for those who have time but no money. Joint ventures are lucrative and can help people invest their money in other things.

There's always a strategy. The more investor support you can offer to them, the more options that they have. You can also offer coaching, letting them know about me. Please let them know I could walk them through this deal every step of the way if they buy it through you. You can let them know I have been in business for over 35 years and know how to do things like fix and flip properties. This way, they can be resourceful and have access to people who can help you with your goals. You can let them know you have also taken care of any objections you may have had, such as cost and financing options, so that you don't have to worry about those. If you feel you don't have enough time, you could consider a joint venture.

What you've done is take away every barrier they could have. You've literally increased the odds that the deal will happen. Get all the contact information for inquiries and detailed reports and to discuss investment strategies.

If you prefer to be contacted by phone calls, please provide your phone number. If you'd rather communicate via email, please let me know your email address.

Unlock the immense potential of 123 Main Street and capitalize on a tailored investment approach. Seize this opportunity for unprecedented returns in the thriving real estate market. Always end with a punch; always pack something meaningful to leave a lasting impression.

Some wholesalers viewing a picture of a house that is literally falling apart may think it is a steal. They then see the other pictures and see the first picture was the worst. Investors are looking for that, they want to know what's wrong, they're not looking for a nice paint job.

They're not looking for a nice rosebush. They're not looking for matching appliances. When they look at the property photos, they want to find fault. They don't see the items; they only see the clutter. For instance, if they come across a hoarder's house, they might only think about the cost of clearing out the stuff and taking it to the dump. However, what concerns them more is what's hidden behind the clutter. They might worry about termite infestation, mold, or other issues. That's why it's crucial to take detailed pictures to capture the essence of the situation.

When contacting potential buyers about a deal under contract, introduce yourself and provide some details about the property you are selling. Let them know you are selling your assignment contract. Give them all the details that you know. If they are showing interest, tell them you have contacts of lenders for them. It's important to be transparent with your investors and share any helpful information with them. Sometimes people are hesitant to share because they worry others will take advantage of their resources. However, the opposite is true-the more resources you have, the more people will want to do business with you. This is because they see that you have the knowledge and expertise to help them succeed. When you do favors for others, there is often a natural tendency for them to want to return the favor. Whether it's by working on a deal together or simply providing support, people want to help those who have helped them.

One important thing that you have done by being resourceful is that now the investor buyer you have helped can be contacted if you have questions or need any help, even outside of a contract. This open dialogue is really nice, and you can become friends. It's usually the same investors that buy and look for properties, so it's a small world. Just be aware of this and inform them that the deposit is $3000 to their lawyer or attorney if they want to commit to the deal.

It's important to inform the other party that the earnest money deposit (EMD) is non-refundable from the outset. The reason for this is that you have already incurred expenses such as the cost of the appraisal, inspector, and contractor quotes. you have invested a lot of time and effort into this, and as such, you cannot afford to have the deal fall through.

We want to make sure we have serious interest; therefore, the $3,000 deposit is needed. If they back out, then they lose their $3,000.

I have provided you with all the information about the property that I could gather. I have walked the property and sent my assistant to do the same. I have also shared detailed pictures of the property with you. I shared with you what I know about the zoning and the location. I have answered all the questions you had. The buyer who visits the property should already have a good idea about everything, so they can just walk in, see the property, and decide in about ten minutes. If I have done my job right, they should not have any questions remaining. That's how smooth it is. Because I've done it, I've witnessed it. I've been the wholesaler and I've been the buyer and that's all that it takes. Investors don't want to waste their time. They have opportunities to look at properties all the time with real estate agents. They don't need to go to wholesalers.

Most real estate agents don't put as much effort into what I'm teaching you right now. Most realtors aren't putting that kind of effort into it. When requesting real estate comparisons from a realtor, it is important to be cautious, as the information provided may not be completely accurate. Often, realtors will provide loose or incomplete comparisons that require further examination. For example, the lot size may be different, or the number of bedrooms or basement may not be the same. These differences can affect the value of the property, and it is important to carefully consider all factors when making comparisons. While realtors are valuable resources, it is important to carefully review all information provided and to clearly understand the comparisons being made.

What I am saying is that the techniques I teach are focused on creating wholesalers who can provide investors with profitable deals. Investors are always on the lookout for good deals, and if you implement my teachings, it increases the chances that an investor will jump on your deal. The aim is to establish credibility so that interested and financially capable buyers can close the deal when the seller agrees. Once the deal is closed, you can set up a meeting between the buyer and the seller at a time that works for both parties.

I won't schedule a viewing unless I know for sure it is ok. Questions I ask the interested Investor buyer: Do you have the $250,000 to acquire the assignable contract in cash? How long will it take you to get it? Alright, it will take you five days. I have seven days left in my contingency condition. There's a non-refundable deposit of $3,000 prior to viewing. If you arrive at the property and it's not exactly as I described it, I will refund your $3,000. But I can assure you that it's exactly as I said it was. This sets the stage that you don't want to waste the seller's time, and you want investors to feel like they were not deceived or coerced.

It's important to respect your seller's time while showing a property to investors. You don't want them to feel like they've been lied to or pressured. The ideal scenario is when an investor shows up with a genuine interest in the property and just wants to verify what they've seen in pictures. I've witnessed investors who, after a quick walkthrough, make an offer on the spot because they were pre-screened and well-informed about the property. To avoid surprises, it's important to disclose all details about the property, both good and bad.

A lot of wholesalers leave out the ugly because they don't want to lose the deal. You will lose the deal, either today or tomorrow, if you're not disclosing everything. It won't close, it will backfire at one stage. What we're doing is when we get to this stage, a new investor buyer is going into the seller's property. They already want the place, and the seller cannot scare, intimidate, or worry them. If the seller moves the carpet and the floor is missing, the investor will say, "Yeah, I already saw that." The investor will know that the property is in full rehab per the inspection report, which will give you credibility.

It's crucial to disclose everything to the buyer to avoid losing the deal. Be transparent to gain credibility and attract serious buyers. Screen potential buyers and only show the property to those who are genuinely interested and qualified.

To ensure that you are dealing with serious buyers and not just casual visitors, it is important to screen them properly. This means that tire kickers may not see the property and only pre-qualified individuals can gain access. These are the steps you should take to pre-qualify buyers. Once they have completed these steps and have been approved, you can then schedule a viewing at a time that has been agreed upon by both the buyer and seller. If you've booked off, say a two-hour timeframe with the seller to show investors, I would suggest you book them half an hour apart. For example, if you have two to four bookings, I will book the first investor at 2:00 p.m., then I would book the second one at 2:30 p.m. Even though I'm there for two hours and the investors have 15 minutes to view the property because I have other investor partners that are coming. Just be upfront with them and inform them of this.

They can look at the property outside from the road anytime they want. However, let them know they need to bring everything to me because as the wholesaler I'm the direct contact. The seller goes through me. If they have questions, I will get them answers. I just need them to visit the property in a non-invasive way and glance at the few things they're concerned about. During the screening process, when they're going through the inspection, they can ask the seller if they have questions based on the inspection. They can tell them they have seen the property or have more pictures and ask if they have any concerns or anything they don't like. It's better to focus on things that make you nervous or that they don't like, rather than things they do like.

Is there anything that would prevent them from proceeding with the deal now that they have seen the inspection report? If there is anything, please inform me so that we can address it properly. For instance, they can let me know the contractor quoted an outrageous amount for a particular repair, or you can ask for more pictures to clarify certain issues. For example, if the inspector mentioned mold in the report, but you noticed it was only up to a certain height of the wall, you can let me know. Please communicate any concerns they may have, and we will work together to find a solution.

When you are dealing with a property inspector, inform them of any issues that you may have noticed. For instance, if the roof needs to be replaced, take a picture of the damage and share it with the inspector. Remember, the inspector is paid to find problems with the property, so be upfront and let them know of any issues. Keep in mind that the inspector is paid at a flat rate, and the more problems they find, the more money you can potentially negotiate off the sale price. If you are selling the assignable contract for the property, let the first buyer know it is first come first served basis. If they are serious about purchasing the property, they will need to make an earnest money deposit, which is non-refundable. Be upfront with them and let them know that if they want to seal the deal, they need to act fast.

Many people struggle with closing a sale. It's important to simply ask the investor if they are taking the deal and then remain silent. We often feel like we need to do all the talking, but it's really about listening to the person's response. You don't have to convince them to buy your assignable contract, you've already presented the information. It's important to keep your emotions in check. Just ask if they are taking the deal and listen to their answer. That's it. They say yes, great, they say no, great, they say, "You keep marketing it; you keep showing it." You only have so many days to remove your contingencies and conditions.

If you're planning to book a property to showcase to potential investors, it's best to have at least three to five pre-screened individuals who will be attending. It's also important to ensure that you've done thorough research and prepared well for the event. As I mentioned before, this is why having a strong buyers list is crucial, as it's challenging to attract enough interested parties. Many prospective buyers may drop out after learning specific details, such as the price, closing date, or the amount of work needed for renovation. Ultimately, what may initially seem like a large pool of potential buyers can quickly become a much smaller group of serious candidates.

It doesn't take long to weed them out because they're not all looking for the same thing. If they're all investors, they might be all looking for fix and flip. Each could still look for totally different things. Sometimes, when working with my partners, there are nine of us on a project and we all have different opinions. It's like herding cats, as each of us looks at the property from different angles. We don't have the same mindset for deciding on the rehab work required. Some consider it a full rehab while others think a cosmetic one is enough. Everyone has their own way of looking at things, so it's important to manage our emotions and keep calm. It's okay if a potential investor buyer rejects an offer after marketing the property. If you don't have any days left, you can go back to the seller and ask if they're open to giving you another 10-14 days. You can also ask the buyers what the reason is for rejecting the deal. The only thing that you can control is the price.

Well, you don't really have control over that, but the only thing that you could do is to negotiate the price. For instance, if the investor buyer made an offer of $275,000 instead of the asking price of $325,000. Depending on your assignment fee, you can go back to the seller and inform them that an investor is interested, but at a lower price. If you still want to make a profit, you can suggest a price of either $225,000 to make $50,000 or $250,000 to make $25,000. It's important to ensure that you make a profit.

You always want to factor in what you're going to get paid. Therefore, negotiate below the asking price. These are some tips and tricks that you can use when negotiating property prices. If you have someone interested in the property, you can negotiate by going back and forth until you agree on a price. If you're unsure about how to negotiate, there are plenty of YouTube videos that can help. You can also simply state that you're a problem solver and that you have an investor who is interested in the property, but only has a certain amount to offer. You can negotiate from a position of leverage, and with the seller's commitment, you can come to an agreement on a price that works for both parties.

What you're going to be leveraging is based on the contractor quotes because our business model is to buy it and fix it up to excellent condition.

If they agree to that, then we've got it done, and the conditions can be removed. Most likely 90% of the time they're going to say let's get it done because that's the closest that they get. Otherwise, you ask for an extension. Plan B is to say I have a few more investors that I haven't heard from them yet regarding the deal, because they're on vacation. Just ask the seller if they can give you another 14 days to satisfy the conditions. If they agree and after 14 days, I still face the same challenge, then it comes down to either getting the deal at a lower price or no deal at all. I'm always willing to work towards making a deal happen and finding a solution. Even if I'm only making $5,000 on a wholesale deal, I'm happy if the seller is satisfied, and the investor buyer is happy. It's all about moving the properties and building up cash flow by finding serious cash buyers.

Facebook Ad Copy to Attract Cash Buyers

https://app.bitly.com/Bo4pjwghIeQ/http://bit.ly/3AlXrTR

Chapter 10

In Chapter 10, things get interesting, as you can see the satisfaction on the investor buyer's face when you have a serious cash buyer. This means that you've done all the research and due diligence to make the deal happen. (You enlisted an inspector, an appraiser, and sent all of this and the buyer's feature sheet to the investor cash buyer.)

Once the investor buyer has said yes, they will provide their name, email, and phone number, as well as the contact information for their attorney or lawyer. It is important to know who their attorney is because they will facilitate the transaction. The only other option for closing a real estate transaction is through a title company. Knowing all this information will help you navigate the process smoothly.

To ensure smooth communication between all parties involved in a real estate transaction, it is advisable to gather the contact information of all parties and have your lawyer contact their lawyer. This will ensure that all necessary paperwork is exchanged, and that everyone is on the same page. It is important to communicate the final sale price to your lawyer, so they can include it in the paperwork. When making an offer, it is crucial to factor in the difference between the purchase price and the final sale price to determine your profit.

That's why the numbers are going to be different. You will want to make sure your investor buyers are aware of what price you're selling your assignable contract at, and what you're buying it for. To summarize selling your assignable contract on a property, the investor buyer will meet at their lawyer's office to sign the offer and then send the signed offer to your lawyer. From this point forward, the title company, lawyers, and attorneys will take care of any necessary paperwork or legal matters to facilitate the sale of the assignable contract. This part of the process is all internal and you won't have to get involved. However, I still recommend monitoring things and staying in contact. Once the conditions are removed, the sale will likely be completed.

Ask your lawyer to draft a copy of the contract that has conditions and contingencies removed. This will allow you to have a document in place that states you have communicated with the buyer and the seller that you're buying the property or that you're assigning that property to someone else.

In previous chapters, we discussed an important document called an assignment clause. This document represents an agreement between you and the investor buyer, stating that the assignment is complete. Once you have a committed investor buyer, you can gather the documents and drafts that will allow you to remove the conditions formerly stated in your offer. These conditions may have included a specific number of days, such as 14 or 30, that you needed to fulfill before closing the deal. By fulfilling these requirements, you have satisfied your obligation to the seller, and the conditions can now be removed. Essentially, this is just fulfilling conditions and removing them from the agreement.

What you have is a contract based on how your lawyer has drafted the documents that are locking in the seller and the investor buyer. It is committing the investor buyer to pay more than what the seller was asking. That difference is given to you by your lawyer. Once you have that document, meet with the seller in person or remotely.

When you sign the removal of the conditions, it is important that you do it in front of the concerned parties. You can even do it remotely but give them a copy of the signed document. As a wholesaler, you need to follow up a lot with the sellers because they may not be well-versed in selling properties. You will need to assist them in every way. When you give them a copy of the signed document, send a copy to their lawyer and also to your lawyer. This way, you ensure you are the one driving the transaction and making it seamless. You will do most of the work.

Most times, the wholesaler is more educated than the seller. They can't do a lot of things on their own. I send the contract with the removal of conditions to my lawyer and the investor buyer's lawyer and the seller's lawyer and copy everyone on the email, so each person is knowledgeable. Sometimes the title company will act on behalf of the seller and the wholesaler.

That's a conversation that you would have with the title company or with the attorney. It all depends on how the seller wishes to proceed, but the goal is to ensure that everything is transparent. Whatever information the seller's lawyer requires, it's crucial to provide it to them. It's not advisable to rely on the seller to communicate the information to their lawyer, as this may cause delays and complications. I am currently working on a deal that has been going on for six and a half months, and we are struggling to get the seller to comply. Unfortunately, we have no control over their actions. As an investor, it can be frustrating, but we need to keep pushing forward and accept that we have more at stake than they do.

Many times, the real money is made from the business of helping people who are moving out of their properties. It is important to offer a high level of support to these individuals, holding their hand and being with them every step of the way. This is especially true because moving can be an emotionally charged experience. The property may hold many memories, or the person may leave behind something that was inherited. It is important to understand these emotions and to be supportive as the person navigates through this challenging time.

It might have been a divorce, an illness, maybe they're aging, usually when we talk to a motivated seller, it's not good. It's not that they're happy about selling the property in all regards. Usually, it's been a burden to them or they need to unlock the cash because of an emergency. It's important to manage both your emotions and those of your seller.

Sometimes you must manage your investor buyer's emotions, since they might get a little frustrated. There might have been a bit of a hiccup that could cause a delay in something. Make sure you stay in contact with them to help ease stress.

Chapter 11

I love this part. Ask for a favor.

Ask for referrals. Who do they know in the same situation? People love to do favors for others; it makes them feel good. So, when someone is going through hard times, such as a marital breakup, they might know other people who are going through that as well.

They might know other family or friends with health concerns, aging, or a need to downsize. They don't have enough money, so they've got to unlock equity.

Whatever their circumstances are, they may know other people who are also struggling. As you're navigating this deal, and as you're getting it from the beginning to the end, or you're getting paid and they're going to move on, they're going to be talking to a lot of people. They will talk to movers, Uber drivers, relatives, co-workers, etc.

When they're about to move, they will engage with new people. They might talk to family members who'll be helping them move. People will know what you're doing for them.

So, ask them who they know. "Who do you know that we can help? Who do you know that's in the same situation as you that we can help?" By putting that bug in their ear and letting them know that you're open to referrals and would assist anyone they know, again, they're grateful for what you're doing. Now, they might not always show that gratitude. They could be disgruntled throughout this entire process. They might need counseling sessions where you're not a counselor, but you will feel like it some days. Just keep in mind that even asking who you know, even if you're feeling like, my goodness, this person's not receptive to this whatsoever.

You'd be surprised, once you just put that thought in there of who do you know, in that moment, they might say I don't know anybody, but they're going to remember. Eventually, by them going ahead and referring someone to you, it will make them feel good as well. The law of reciprocation is that you did something for them, and they want to return the favor. As this is navigated, they're going to realize you facilitated it. It might not be the best situation, and they might not be the happiest because of the situation. Still, the biggest thing is that once they feel that relief, which might be during this transaction, it might be at the end of this transaction, once it's closed, and they've got the money when suddenly, the pressure is off them. In those moments, they might talk to someone, maybe three or six months later.

I had one deal that I did. And six months later, the seller reached out to me and said, "You know, I have a friend in the same position I was in." So, you never know, as you're navigating this, and you're next to them, and you're staying close to them, and I know I use the term babysitting, but the reality of it is that there's a fire, and they don't know how to get to the exit, all you're doing is getting them to the exit. So they don't know what they're doing, they're so emotionally distraught.

I'd say 99% of the of the people that we deal with are so distraught that they're not thinking clearly. They're not able to decide or execute things. You must do that.

They're going to feel that even though a lot is going on, it's chaotic, they're going to feel that the seller will become a raving fan, the more people that we can go out there and help through wholesaling, helping the sellers who are panic sellers, they're distraught, don't know what they're doing; and have this enormous asset, and they don't know how to manage it for whatever reason. Now, couple that with an investor buyer, and you've held their hand through this entire process. That's how a raving fan is developed.

That's how you develop your reputation. That's why I recommend getting a website. Now they have a place to go and can see what you're all about.

Chapter 12

Chapter 12 is about the follow through. This matter is crucial. Please let the seller know they need to contact their lawyer for advice on what their next steps should be. This is not something that can be handled by anyone else but the seller themselves. They need to get advice on that. It's important to keep in touch with your title company, lawyer, or attorney during the process of any legal transaction. You should remind them constantly about their next steps and ask how you can assist them. For example, you might suggest to them they need to provide their bank information for receiving payment or meet with you to sign the required documents. By staying in communication with them and guiding them through the steps, you can ensure that everything goes smoothly and according to plan.

If you're selling your assignable contract for a property, there might be some steps that need to be taken care of before the purchase can be completed. One way to speed up the process is to talk to your lawyer and ask them what needs to be done. Your lawyer can then communicate with the seller's lawyer to figure out what's causing the delay. While they're doing that, you can ask your lawyer to keep you updated on what the seller needs to do to move things forward. This way, you can stay informed and make sure the assignment goes smoothly.

That is where you come into play. If you want, you can speak to the seller and offer assistance in case their lawyers are waiting for them at the time of signing. You could offer to pay for their transportation, such as an Uber or a taxi, if needed. If they miss work on the day of signing, you could consider offering them an additional $100 on the closing date to compensate for the lost time.

I'm asking you to tap into your creativity. Do you remember when we first started working together? We talked about mindset and being in a positive state of mind. When you approach a situation with a powerful mindset, your perspective changes. Instead of thinking negatively about the seller, you can ask yourself, *How can I help them? What can I do to facilitate this deal? What actions are within my control?* You can send an email, a text, or make a phone call. You can even bring in additional resources if necessary. Being resourceful and proactive will help you achieve your goals and maintain a positive state of mind.

As you gain more resources, you'll be in a better state financially. However, it's important to keep in mind that you shouldn't always hand over the responsibility to the seller. Instead, follow up and ask if they spoke with their lawyer and what the next steps are. You can also check if there are any pending requirements that need to be fulfilled. It's essential to inform the sellers that their lawyer will receive the money on the closing date. Once the documents are signed, and all the contingencies are removed, the offer becomes unconditional, and it's a done deal. The only thing left is the exchange of money.

When you're explaining the process to the sellers, it's important to emphasize that their lawyer is their best ally. The lawyer is the one who will hold their money and ensure that it's available on the closing date that was agreed upon. To avoid any confusion or frustration, it's a good idea to communicate clearly with the sellers and provide them with all the information. Give them the reassurance they need by letting them know that their money will wait for them at the lawyer's office on the agreed-upon date. If the sellers continue to ask about the money, you can direct them to their lawyer, who will provide them with all the details on how to access it.

Everything has to be done legally, and it must be documented. You need to stay in touch with the seller every third day until the closing date. Ask them if they need any support with their move and provide them as many resources as you can. Regardless of the communication method, sellers rarely return calls because they are shy or they don't want to ask for help or, in a lot of cases, they are embarrassed by this situation.

With that being said, all we can do is do our part and stay in touch with the sellers, letting them know we're here for them.

We can ask them if the movers are still scheduled to arrive on time? Is the rental truck still available for that day? Did everything go well with the dumpster delivery, especially since you plan on getting rid of stuff? Do you need me to call someone for you? If you don't have any movers, don't worry. I know some and can provide you with a backup plan. It's always a good idea to get to know people in the city, such as realtors, appraisers, inspectors, and other professionals. You can also research and find movers.

The more resources you have, the more resourceful you can be with this seller and your chances of the deal successfully closing goes up. Until the seller moves and gives up vacant possession, the deal will not come together. Even though there is a legal contract, there's still no guarantee until the seller gets their money, and you get yours. During this time, maintaining a relationship with someone can be compared to a dance. You need to stay committed to them, regardless of any challenges that arise. This means staying in touch and being there for them, no matter what they're going through or how they're feeling. I want to emphasize that this doesn't mean you should constantly call them, but if they're open to texting, you can check in and offer your help if needed.

Even put yourself in their shoes so you have a better way to relate to them. For example, acknowledge that it must be hard to pack up this house they have lived in for a long time. A gracious gesture would be to offer to call some people to assist them with packing.

It is always nice to be compassionate and offer a personal touch. Even though this is a business transaction, it is affecting these people's lives and the more you put yourself in their shoes, you will have a better understanding and not take things personally when there are bad days. There will be better days than some.

There are different people, different lawyers, different sources, and influences that are always coming into the mix. You will need to navigate this like a marriage to make it all come together. However, the lawyers will have the final say.

The important thing is to stay in constant contact with the investor buyer, the seller, and your lawyer so you can resolve any challenges and have a successful closing. It's important to remember that there is an investor buyer involved. Thus, maintain regular communication with the investor buyer to ensure that the funds will be available at the lawyer's office on the closing date.

You're ensuring the seller is trustworthy and reassuring them while also seeking reassurance from the investor buyer. All the while, you are also communicating status to the lawyer. You want to make sure the transaction goes smoothly.

There could be up to three other moving parts as far as legalities go, and this is where it can get overwhelming. For managing your emotions, sometimes it may not seem worth the money. For me, sometimes I've thought to myself that the hassle is just too much-the seller isn't cooperating, or the investor buyer isn't cooperating.

I am currently facing some challenges with the lawyers who are not responding to my calls, which is making things difficult for me. However, I need to refocus and regroup myself. I have to ensure that I am in a good state of mind and feeling confident. I must also acknowledge that my services are valuable, and the seller needs my assistance. This seller has approached me either through a Google ad, a mail-out, a referral, or a note put in the door. This client requires my services to move on with their lives.

Is it going to be sticky? Sometimes? Yes. Is it going to be more complicated than it needs to be? Yes. It is important to understand that when you purchase or sell or wholesale a property for the first time, there are a lot of emotions involved, such as investor buyer's remorse and seller's remorse. Investor buyer's remorse is when a buyer doubts their decision after removing the conditions and waiting for the closing date. They might think that this was a bad move and feel scared about it, figuring out a way to get out of it. However, this is less likely to happen with an investor because they have done it enough times.

Some people experience seller's remorse after making a sale. They may suddenly feel unsure if they made the right decision and become overwhelmed by the process. Sometimes, just speaking with a lawyer can be too much for them to handle. These individuals may avoid conversations and bury their heads in the sand, not because they are being difficult, but because they are scared, uneducated, and emotional. They are doing something they do not want to do, and external factors in their lives may force their hand. It is important to remember what they are going through and approach the situation with empathy.

It is good to be aware of this. I often say to my students, we're not investors in real estate, we're investors in people. This is a people business. The better and more authentic you can become with people, coming from a place of helping them, the more successful you will be at helping them. The result is that you will be rewarded with a payment. I am inspired a lot by Jim Rohn, Tony Robbins, and Darren Hardy. I watch a lot of their YouTube videos. I also have a couple of coaches myself. I need their guidance because hearing constant problems and solving other people's problems can weigh heavily on me after a while.

When you're helping people solve their problems or creating solutions for them, it can be a heavy burden. So, before you decide to take on such a responsibility, be aware of what you're signing up for. However, with practice, you can become skilled at it and be there for people when they need you. Unfortunately, some people in the business world just focus on making quick money without caring about the seller's needs. This approach is wrong and can lead to bad karma. When I'm looking at a deal, I always ask myself if I'm helping the seller. If the answer is yes, then I proceed with the deal.

If I am successful with this, I will be compensated. The first thing I must remember is that I am assisting a seller who is in a position where they may not have the resources to market or fix up their property. If they had access to a realtor or the funds, they wouldn't need my help. It's important to acknowledge that they need my expertise to navigate the process and guide them through it. One seller I am currently working with prefers to communicate via text, and I find that to be the most effective means of communication. As I guide him through the process, I remind him of what needs to be done next and encourage him to act.

Sometimes I can't even assume that it's simple, that it is common sense. "You know what? Just do this." Finally, I suggested to the gentleman, "Would it be better if I send you a list of things that you need to do?" He responded with a resounding, "Yes!" I instructed him step by step on how to send the fax. He needed to find the nearest place to send it, print out the document, sign on line one, line five, and line ten, and then fax it to the phone number. Finally, he was asked to send me a text message to confirm that the process was complete. I broke it down for him, explaining each step one by one.

It ended up being 11 steps. It was a matter of him being overwhelmed; he clearly couldn't think straight. Normally, in this situation, I would have told him to go there, send the fax, and be done with it. But I could tell that he was stressed and very emotional. As I communicated with him and connected with him, I realized what he needed from me. He wanted to fulfill his obligations and do his part, but he just didn't know what to do or in what sequence to do it.

I've gone and dropped off notes in someone's mailbox before, and they've come out yelling at me, saying I had no right to put a note in their mailbox. There are days when you're not someone's favorite person, and there are people who are upset. I remember there was one woman I was helping, and she gave me a big hug, but the day before, someone was yelling at me. There's a lot of emotion to manage, and it's really important not to take any of it personally. You just have to realize where it's coming from.

When you take a child to a grocery store, you might notice that all the junk food and chocolate bars are placed at eye level for them. Because of this, the child might want to have one. However, when you refuse to buy it for them, they might throw a tantrum and get mad at you.

Perhaps you are taking care of a child who is comfortable following instructions. However, my child wasn't like that. For instance, when I asked them to eat vegetables, or when I told them it was suppertime, it required a constant exchange of negotiations. I had to constantly bargain with them, saying things like "Yes, you can have that toy, but only if you eat your vegetables first." Similarly, when dealing with real estate, around 20% of what you need to do is just common sense. You negotiate with the seller for a reasonable price, find an investor buyer who will pay more, and then you earn a profit. It's like a constant bartering process, where you need to be constantly negotiating and making deals to succeed.

If I was teaching a program just on that, I'd have been done in less than a minute, because really, that is the gist of it. 20% of what we do is the actual work, while the remaining 80% involves managing ourselves and the psychology of the people we interact with. It's important to consider how we present ourselves and how our personal lives may affect our work. For instance, we may deal with personal issues, such as a flat tire or a recent argument with a loved one. It's crucial to be mindful of what we bring to the table when we communicate with others, whether it's through a phone call or a text message. Are we coming off abrasive? Are we angry that day? Are we coming from a good, happy place ourselves?

If we're facing multiple challenges in our life, we need to expand our mind and keep ourselves in check. Even when we have multiple deals on the go simultaneously, whether it's five, ten, or fifteen, the formula remains the same. We need to stay positive, present ourselves well, and navigate every situation with a positive attitude. We can ask questions like "How are you?" and "What do you need from me?" in a friendly tone and with our hands on our hips to show confidence. By keeping ourselves in check and maintaining a positive mindset, we can tackle any challenge that comes our way.

There have been many days in my experience where I had to *fake it to make it*. Despite having personal issues going on in my life, I had to put on my best face and show up as my best self. When someone would ask me how I was doing, I would respond with positivity, such as "I'm awesome. How are you today?" However, if I was dealing with a seller who was going through a tough time, I wouldn't want to make them feel inferior by saying I'm fantastic. So, I would respond with "I'm well, thank you. How can I help you today?" or "I'm blessed. How are you?" My response would depend on the connection I wanted to have with the seller.

Emotions are riding even higher than they were now that we're getting down to crunch time and close to the closing date. The fear is kicking in for them. The insecurities are kicking in too. The doubts come in and they may ask themselves, *did I do something wrong? Oh, should I have done this? Where am I going to go? Is it going to be okay? People where I'm going don't agree with my decision. Am I going to make the same mistake that just happened?*

I understand that once someone sells their property, the pain point that led them to this decision disappears; however, a new pain may arise. Many sellers don't take personal development or counseling, and they may end up unloading their emotions on you. Personally, I prefer it when someone expresses their thoughts and feelings, even if they are yelling or changing their mind. I find it better than dealing with someone who is unresponsive. After working in this field for a long time, I can usually tell when a person is going to have an outburst or when something is about to happen.

A few months ago, I facilitated a transaction for a couple. During the process, I only communicated with the wife, and everything seemed to be going well. All the checks were done, and we were able to get another investor on board. The deal was closed, and it was actually my birthday, and I was out for dinner with my family and my phone rang. It was the husband calling me, furious that he was not included in the process. He accused me of not talking to him and not going through him. I was taken aback because I had been communicating with his wife for two months and I assumed he had my number and could have called me at any time. I want to clarify that I am always available and transparent in my dealings.

He was really upset with me. I thought I did him a favor, so he should be happy instead of angry. I tried to listen to him when the server came to take my payment. He could tell that I was out for dinner. He said he would call me tomorrow, and I agreed. What I didn't mention earlier is that it was my birthday. I had steak for dinner with my husband and father, but I couldn't eat it while it was still hot because I was getting yelled at.

Imagine the state I'm in. I'm in a good place right now. I'm out for my birthday dinner, feeling happy and celebrating getting a year younger. I've decided that I'm going back the other way now. I was taking a call at the restaurant because of the closing date of something important. They had even moved the closing date to my birthday. I was determined to finish everything before my birthday so that I wouldn't have to work on my special day. The lawyers were causing a lot of problems. The deal had already gone past the closing dates, and the lawyers were not doing their job properly. It was a complete mess, with so many things happening at once. I had to manage the emotions of the lawyers and their co-signers. It was a lot to handle.

I was very invested in the entire process as an investor buyer, and my heart went out to the family involved because they were going to be homeless for Christmas. I was emotional and wanted to help, but I had to make sure that everything was secure for the investor. Navigating all of this was a challenge, and on my birthday, I expected a quick 30-second call just to thank me for my help. However, it turned out to be a lot more complicated than that. Overall, there were many challenges that I had to overcome to make sure that everything was okay.

There were three lawyers involved in the transaction. The properties were not in my city or my province. Because of the bad weather, some people couldn't get to the location to sign the documents. There were many emotions involved in the process, making it complicated. I had not seen the property myself, but there were many people involved, and it had many moving parts. Despite all these challenges, I am happy to say the transaction was successful, and the clients were going to be okay. Knowing that they would have a great Christmas made me feel like I had done my part in solving their problem.

Keep in mind I was busy enjoying myself when suddenly this guy called me up and sounded upset and was yelling at me. I listened to him while thinking in my head that it was my birthday and I didn't want to deal with it. I was wondering why he wasn't grateful, but I know I need to be professional and compassionate no matter what. I have internal dialogue in moments like this, but I've learned not to say everything I'm thinking. While he was talking, I reminded myself to manage my state and thought about what I can do to handle the situation.

What did I want to say? I apologize, but you can't blame me for something I didn't do (they were facing the power of sale and sheriff eviction prior to my involvement). I did say sorry for the way you feel, but it wasn't my fault. He thinks it shouldn't have happened that way, but I was not involved in it. I had a Zoom meeting with him and his wife, and that was the last I heard from him. Did I miss something?

You don't know what's going on in that house. You don't know what's really going on in someone else's world. I didn't take it personally but could not help but feel upset as I was boxing up my meal, feeling upset and unable to eat. This person spent about 20 minutes downloading their thoughts and feelings on me, and I just listened.

It ended with, I'm going to call you. He never called back. There was something going on in his world.

I told him I strongly believe his wife would attest to the fact that I always answer my phone. As a wholesaler, I maintain high standards of integrity. Even if I didn't expect the call to be a good one, it's important to me to be available to the seller, who may need to reach out to me.

I'll tell you what happens when I receive a call, even if I don't want to take it. I answer the phone and say, 'Theresa speaking, may I help you?' even though I don't feel like it. Despite my reluctance, I still make money from the transaction, and I have earned it. However, the person on the other end of the line may not be happy with my service. I understand that he may have other problems and issues that I can't help with, but I solved one problem for him. Unfortunately, I cannot solve everything for him. This has nothing to do with real estate, this has nothing to do with me. So, that's the message I really want to impress upon you- be the person who answers the phone, even if things aren't going well or if it's not convenient. For example, on my birthday, I did not want to talk to anybody about anything. I just wanted to have an enjoyable meal.

It's important for me that people know that I'm here for them. Even when it's my birthday, it wouldn't have been appropriate to tell someone who was very upset to call me back later. I'm not saying that you should bring your phone to dinner with your family or during celebrations, but let's imagine a scenario where I left my phone in the car during my birthday dinner. If I later noticed a missed call and returned it after dinner, I might be caught off guard by the caller's anger.

I am now calling back the number because I didn't listen to my message first. When I called, the person on the other end got angry with me. What I learned from this experience is that regardless of when you make a call, whether you answer your phone right away or check your voicemail first, you need to manage yourself. It doesn't matter if you've had experience with door-to-door sales, like I have, or if you've sold cemetery plots, vacuums or worked as a telemarketer. You need to understand where you're at and be mindful of the impact of your actions.

I've done a lot of different things. I was a school bus driver. There were 72 screaming kids while I was driving. I've gone through some different jobs and opportunities. As a bartender, your experiences merge into one, and you never know when they'll come in handy. Whether it's helping others or getting into the real estate business, life can surprise you in unexpected ways.

I encourage you to be a good person. Being a good person not only benefits you morally but also financially. Perhaps you're tired of living paycheck to paycheck or you want to generate wealth and make a significant income. Whatever your goals may be, you need to become fantastic at what you do and understand it inside out. Once you've gained that level of expertise, you can achieve anything you set your mind to, whether it's making $50,000, $100,000, or even

$200,000 a year or more. Keep pushing yourself and strive to be the best version of yourself.

At the beginning of the book, I asked what are you listening to? What are you watching? You will need to have a certain set of skills to deal with people effectively. Even the lawyers involved in the transaction may not have the best communication skills. Similarly, sellers and investors may not be easy to deal with. As a wholesaler, it's important to be the most resourceful and level-headed person in the transaction. No matter what happens, I need to stay calm and in control. These skills are crucial at this stage of the transaction because the stakes are high, and the outcome is uncertain.

Yes, there is a contract. However, I've had sellers back out at the last minute, and the deal dies. I'm not saying that it's happened often in my career, but is it possible? Yes. What are you going to do? Sue? Sue a panic seller? Probably not. It's important to manage these things, as it will make things easier. The more you can manage a seller, the more investors will want to deal with you. This is because they will see what's going on.

If it was easy, everybody would do it. Wholesaling isn't for the faint at heart, you have to have some thick skin. You must constantly stay in touch with the investor buyer. You need to contact them every other day, ensuring that all is going as planned, that the funds are being sent to your lawyer, and that they're going to go to their lawyer. If they need any support or if there are any issues, you need to know immediately.

You will want to check in and make sure that the investor buyer is still on track to send all the money to your lawyer.

It's important that everything is going according to plan and that your lawyer is connecting with the investor buyer's lawyer to ensure that everything is on the same page. If there are any issues, please stress this to your lawyer so that they can address it immediately. We need to know if there is nothing happening when it should be.

Your lawyer needs to know if there's a hiccup with the seller's lawyer, or the investor buyer's lawyer, or the seller or the buyer. You need to know immediately because you're the go between and you're the one that has developed a relationship with that seller and with the investor buyer. You are the only one most times that can rectify an issue that's going to come up. It's often just a matter of having a conversation. Sometimes a little more or less money can resolve the problem.

The biggest challenge for selling an assignable contract for a property is often the investment of resources like money, time, and effort. As a seller, it can be a struggle to deal with the pain of letting go of a property, while as an investor buyer, there's the excitement of a new beginning. Investor buyers are often eager to connect every other day, as they are looking forward to the pleasure of moving in and getting started with construction, utility switching, and money management. As I mentioned in the first chapter, the two primary motivators behind buying and selling are pain and pleasure.

You have a seller who is motivated to sell because of the pain they are experiencing, which can come with a lot of emotional baggage. You have an investor buyer who is enthusiastic about the purchase. As the middleman, it's important to maintain a balance between the two parties.

You need to be enthusiastic when speaking to the investor buyer, but remain neutral when dealing with the seller.

It is important to be sensitive about the situation when dealing with lawyers. They may not be as invested in the deal as you are, as they have multiple clients to attend to. Therefore, it is crucial to stay on top of the deal and ensure that everything is being taken care of properly. Your reputation is at stake and this deal is of utmost importance to you.

When you email all three lawyers, you need to know that you are the facilitator. You should immediately be notified of anything that comes up, and you will take care of it. This is an ongoing process and not a one-time event. Don't assume that sending one email is enough and that everything will go smoothly. Even if the investor buyer says that everything is going as planned, you still need to stay on top of things and be proactive. Only then can you relax and wait for payday, knowing that the closing date will come, and everything will be good.

It does not happen that way. When dealing with real estate, it's common for realtors to manage their emotions until the closing date to receive their commission. As wholesalers, we sell contracts and not real estate, which often comes with its own set of challenges. However, being resourceful and knowing where to turn to solve any problems that arise is key. Most times, there are only a few outcomes, and if you're aware of what they are, you'll be better equipped to handle any issues that may arise.

It is rare for people to change their minds. In fact, it only happens once in every 100 to 200 deals, or even one in every 500 deals. When you come across such a situation, anticipate it, as it is highly unlikely to happen. To give you an analogy, it's like playing video games where the players shoot at each other. Although it might not be the best example, I have observed my son playing it for years.

He could navigate through any environment while shooting and being alert. He could predict someone around the corner, based on the building's layout and the position of the corners. He could expect potential problems and keep a watchful eye on them. My goal with this program is to enable you to be aware of your surroundings and anticipate any issues.

I am not here to tell you that everything will be easy and perfect if you take this course. Making money or achieving success facing no challenges is not what I am promoting. If you already have the skills to handle a transaction that goes completely smoothly, you don't need this book. My aim is to help you handle challenges and overcome obstacles that may come your way in your journey towards success.

When you're anticipating a conversation with someone about a potential move, there are several factors to consider. For instance, there's a possibility that someone might come out from the right or the left, or they might have something to say about movers and the closing date. They could also mention that their kids, parents, spouse, or even they themselves are sick, and thus they've missed time off work. To make matters worse, they might have lost their job in the middle of all this, or they might move to a different city, state, or even country.

There are many things that can go wrong during the moving process. However, if you take the time to get to know the potential challenges, you can anticipate and prepare for them. You could ask: Mr. Seller, can you confirm if everything is still on track with the movers? Are they able to move you across the country? Have you confirmed with them? If not, would it be easier for me to send them an email on your behalf? I know you have a lot going on, with packing and everything, and this is a big move for you. If they don't move out of the property, the deal falls through. There is no reason this has to happen. To ensure smooth navigation, it's important to anticipate the concerns of the investor buyer. They may worry about the possibility of the lender not meeting their closing date. To address this, confirm with the investor buyer that everything is on track with their lender. I would recommend resolving any issues with the lender before removing the conditions with the investor buyer.

Are you aware of the property's current condition? It's not just about the money coming in, but also about other factors that need to be taken into consideration. When selling to the investor buyer, it's important to offer your assistance and ask if there is anything you can do to facilitate the process. This can be a stressful time for them, with many moving parts involved. Even if they decline your offer, continue to provide support by asking how else you can be of service.

When selling something, there might be a tendency for the buyer to turn down the offer. However, if you approach the situation intending to serve the investor buyer and continuously asking what else you can do to help, you might eventually hear them say, "Could you take care of this?" This is when you can confidently respond with, "I'm on it!" and they will know that you are committed to helping them.

Moving on, the day before closing can be a crucial time. It's important to anticipate any potential issues and take steps to prevent them. This means ensuring that the lender has the funds, communicating with lawyers, and connecting with the seller and buyer to confirm everything is on track. A lot can happen the day before closing, so it's essential to be prepared.

Suddenly, things go completely sideways. If there is something that's going sideways, you have time the day before closing. Most times, you can rectify whatever's going on. The day before the closing, email your lawyer and confirm all is going as planned. They have already communicated with the investor buyer's lawyer. Therefore, it is important for you to communicate with your lawyer at this point. Your lawyer is the one who is working for you and earning their fee. You should confirm with your lawyer if everything is going as planned, if the money is being transferred as expected, and if everything is good to go.

It's important to stay informed throughout the process of closing a deal. To ensure this, it's recommended that you maintain regular contact with your lawyer. While it is necessary to keep in contact with your lawyer every third day at least, it is critical that you connect with them the day before closing. You need to know what's left to be done, what the lawyer needs from you, and what hasn't been completed yet. The most important thing is to ensure that funds are in place, and that all parties involved have signed the documents. On the day of closing, it's crucial that the money is transferred to the lawyer, and that all the parties involved have signed the required documents. You will have a smooth closing if you keep in touch with your lawyer during the entire process.

Check in with your sellers and offer any assistance, like getting them a meal while they pack. Moving is so hard so any help you can give them is appreciated and strengthens your relationship.

It can be overwhelming when packing and moving. It's easy to lose track of where your food or next meal is going to come from. You can ask the sellers if there is anything you can do to help. I want to ease the pressure they're going through. It's not about making more money, it's about treating others with respect and dignity. We're all human and we never know where we'll end up in life. Treat these people how you would want your mother to be treated. When you come from a place of genuine care and concern, it's not salesy or work, it's just being a decent human being. The sellers are depending on you to close the transaction, even though an investor buyer will take over. They trust you as their point of contact.

They're trusting you; they're putting really their life in your hands. To ensure that the seller is safe, it's important to double-check and cross all your t's and dot all your i's. You must communicate with everyone involved in the process to guarantee that everything is okay. It's suggested to email your lawyer frequently to ensure that there is a paper trail of all the communication. You can ask your lawyer about the progress and funds.

It's important to always be prepared for unexpected situations when dealing with real estate transactions. You never know when things might become challenging, so it's crucial to anticipate potential problems and be resourceful. Emotions can run high on both ends, and lenders may make last-minute changes. The closing date may need to be rescheduled because of the seller's or investor buyer's needs. By staying informed and connected, you can address these challenges before they become major issues. The sooner you identify the problem, the faster you can work towards a solution.

Chapter 13

In Chapter 13, it's important to be aware of all the details involved in closing a deal. Make sure you've confirmed with the investor buyer and your lawyer that everything is in order. It's crucial to have been communicating regularly with your lawyer, the seller, and the investor buyer leading up to the closing day so that there are no surprises. You should have addressed any issues at least a day before the closing to avoid any last-minute complications. Remember, it's always better to be safe than sorry!

On the day of closing, we need to ensure that everything goes smoothly. We should meet early at nine o'clock in the morning when businesses open. As a wholesaler, you play a crucial role. Your talents, drive, due diligence, and follow-up make deals come together. Without you, deals might not happen, or they might rely on luck. We don't want to base our business on luck; we prefer to know what's going on. So, let's focus on our responsibilities and make sure we do our best to close the deal successfully.

Once that's confirmed, contact the seller and let them know again to call their lawyer for instructions because now they're going to want to know when they get their money so they can pay the movers. Most times, the sellers are bugging you before the closing date. Keep reassuring them by explaining that it will be at their lawyer's office, it will be at the title company's office, on the day of closing.

In the meantime, let them know everything is going accordingly as planned. It's like a tap dance. Be knowledgeable. I understand it's scary to make a call, but ignoring it won't solve the problem. Just remember, as long as there is a willing investor, buyer, and seller, the contract will sell and close. Your role is to facilitate this transaction, like a boat floating along in the ocean.

When there is a storm, all you need to do is adjust your sails. If someone comes to you with a problem, ask them what they need to solve it and what their plan is. If your lawyer identifies a problem, ask them what needs to happen and who makes it happen.

Ask what the problem is and what the solution is. When you meet the investor buyer with the lawyer, it's best to start with a positive attitude and ask questions such as "What can we do to move forward? What are the next steps? What can you do? What can I do? What can they do?" Brainstorm different ways to make the transaction successful. The only problem that can arise is if the seller can't move because there's not enough money, or if the investor buyer doesn't come through with the money. However, if you have followed the steps I have outlined, you should be well-prepared for closing day. On that day, it's important to double, triple, and even quadruple check everything to ensure that everything goes smoothly.

Once your lawyer confirms everything is good to go and the funds are ready, you need to inform the seller to call their lawyer, attorney, or title company to get instructions for the payment. This is what you have been working for and the reason you have been putting all your efforts into this. Finally, it's time for pay day! Take a moment to get to where you can celebrate. Email your lawyer and ask them to call you once you can pick up your check.

You can also have them wire the funds to your account, but they charge an extra fee for that. It's usually $50-$100. Normally, deals don't close until after four on the closing date. If you're negotiating a closing date for a property purchase, it's important to keep a few things in mind. For example, you might schedule the closing date just before a long weekend when lawyers are often inundated with many deals and things can get overlooked. It's a good idea to discuss potential closing dates with the seller and come to an agreement together. Keep in mind that sometimes sellers may already have a date in mind, which may not be ideal for you. So, be prepared to negotiate and find a mutually beneficial arrangement.

If you're going into a long weekend, brace yourself, because sometimes things go really sour really fast and they get pushed over after a long weekend. I'm just giving you a heads up. Talk to your lawyer or attorney about that when you put the deal in. Ask them if they anticipate a problem with that date? For example, on June 10th, there are no holidays, but if that date will cause any issues if it's selected for something important, make it convenient for a lawyer. Are there any challenges you expect for that day, week, or month? When should I be mindful of the calendar dates that might cause problems? Is there a particular time of year that's especially busy for you, where you might have a lot of closings all at once? Essentially, I'm asking if you're being proactive in your planning.

By being mindful of potential challenges, you can better mitigate any issues that may arise during the deal. It's important to remember that the celebration of success should come after receiving payment. Take a moment to reflect on why you started this venture and what experiences or feelings you hoped to achieve. Even if you didn't make a large profit on your first deal, consider allocating 20% of it towards something that brings you fulfillment. As Tony Robbins once said, success without fulfillment is the ultimate failure.

You don't want to reach a point in a transaction where you decide to keep all the money and repeat the same action. Eventually, just having money won't be enough. I've talked to many people who have a lot of money, yet they're still unhappy. Some might wonder how that's possible, but trust me, it happens. They lack fulfillment, and they're only focused on increasing the digits in their bank accounts.

Whether you donate to a food bank or at your place of worship, or take your family out for dinner, it's important to take some time to celebrate your accomplishments. Perhaps you have spent little time with your friends lately because of your focus on your wholesaling courses and making offers, so why not invite them over to celebrate closing your first deal? Remember, it's not all about the grind. It's important to share the love and enjoy the journey.

Are you considering taking a day off from work? You can speak to your boss and request a long weekend, starting from Sunday and lasting until Tuesday. Alternatively, take an entire week off for a much-needed vacation or a staycation. The idea is to think outside the box and plan your time off accordingly. Many of us work hard every day, clocking in and out, and putting in long hours, often with little appreciation or recognition. However, taking some time off can help you recharge and come back to work with renewed energy. Why not consider taking some time off and enjoying a well-deserved break?

I remember going to Texas a few years back to see Darren Hardy. During that visit, he challenged us by saying that every time we engage in a money-making activity, we should track our time. I thought it would mean working 18 hours a day.

When I realized that my money-making activities were limited to speaking with sellers, I reassessed the time I was spending on these activities. Typically, I would speak to one seller daily for approximately 45 minutes, as I believe building rapport is important. If I had to speak to an investor buyer, it would take an additional 10 minutes. It was only then that I realized how little time I was dedicating towards money-making activities, as opposed to simply checking emails.

Keep that in mind as you celebrate and realize how hard you had to work. I understand that you have taken this course for a reason, even though I am not aware of your profession. However, I know that many students, just like you, seek financial freedom, more income, and stability. They want to secure their future and be free from the fear of losing their job or not getting a promotion. They wish to have a steady source of income, even when they decide to start a family or buy a house. Robert Kiyosaki calls this *the rat race*, and many people want to find a way out of it.

These are the things to celebrate when you receive a check in your hand. It's proof that the income is real. Your first check could be $5,000. If you challenge yourself to double it, your next check could be $10,000. Then you could aim for $20,000 and $40,000. Finally, you could double it again to $80,000. As you gain experience, you will learn which deals are worth your time and which aren't. It takes time and practice, so expect to look at least 100 deals before you can spot a good one in 15 minutes. With my 35 years of experience, I'm confident that my course will help you achieve your goals.

It took me 35 years to learn this. I can shorten your curve. It will not take you 35 years to learn. I know that it's going to take time, and that's going to depend on you and how serious are you about making this happen for yourself? How committed are you to achieving your goal? How badly do you want to succeed in real estate? Keep in mind that many people are making money in real estate every day. This is happening all around you, and you know it, or you wouldn't have clicked to buy this book.

If you believed that real estate sucks and you knew it would not work, you wouldn't be here. The main point I'm making is that the only thing that separates you from a highly successful wholesaler is time. Once you have identified your niche and your city, and have a good understanding of the market, you can begin to locate and target potential buyers. The key is to find motivated sellers, negotiate with them, and leverage your website and ads to drive customers to you. As you build your buyer's list and gain confidence in your abilities, you'll be able to quickly identify good deals and close them successfully. Ultimately, by focusing on your niche and being strategic in your approach, you'll be able to succeed in the highly competitive world of wholesaling.

It's important to realize who helped you along the way. It is nice to give the contractors that provided you a quote, a gift card for a pizza lunch or tickets to a game. You want them to know that they are valued. It's about spreading the love.

Contractors may question why they're receiving something without having completed a job yet.

I want to encourage them and let them know that because of the quote they shared; I could boost my confidence and successfully sell my contract. If they find a motivated seller for you, you can offer them a gift card or a pizza lunch as a reward.

To let the contractor know they are more valuable than that, you can offer them a monetary reward of $500, $1000, or $5000, depending on the size of the deal.

In the real estate world, a *bird dog* is someone who finds leads for you. You can ask a contractor to become a *bird dog* and find leads for you. You should agree on a payment amount with the contractor. For instance, you can pay them $5,000 if they bring you a lead, as long as you can make $20,000 on it. It's important to establish this beforehand because contractors are not used to this arrangement. Don't forget to thank the investor buyer who helped you secure the deal. You can send them a gift card for materials, a mover, or a cleaner. Without their help, you wouldn't have been able to close the deal on time.

If you aim to please the investor buyer, consider following up with them after sending the gift card or any other gift. It's important to ensure that the gift is delivered successfully, and that the investor buyer is satisfied with the product or service. What's the timeframe when they're going to be done fixing and flipping that property? What's their intention? Are they planning to sell the property once they have a tenant or keep it for a long-term investment? Do they have a specific timeframe in mind? We need to know this information to ask our next question, which is how soon they want another deal like this. For instance, if the investor buyer says they will be ready in 60 days, how soon do you want another deal?

It seems like you have a situation where you already have a buyer in 60 days. Therefore, you have 2 months to find a motivated seller and repeat the process. You can ask the investor buyer if they are interested in buying multiple properties simultaneously, as some investor buyers purchase one to five properties simultaneously with the help of multiple contractors and crews. If you want to work with such a buyer, it's best to learn more about their strategies, buying criteria, and preferences. You should pay attention to what they want and do everything in your power to find properties that fit their buying criteria. This way, you can ensure a successful closing, with no problems, and get paid.

I understand we are in a relationship, and I have delivered what I promised with proof. I know they signed the contract and made the payment, which is what keeps the business going. Following up is crucial for success, and we must meet the seller at their new location or arrange for delivery. The seller has been through a tough time with moving, address changes, and other challenges. They may have experienced movers not showing up, weather, or difficulty fitting all their belongings in their new place. They may have had to throw some things away, and some items may have been broken during the move.

They've gone through a lot. It's important to consider what you can give someone that would make them feel appreciated and valued. This could be anything from an outdoor plant to a gift card for a spa day if they enjoy pampering. If they've recently purchased a new home, a gift card to a hardware store could be a thoughtful idea. Alternatively, if they've expressed the importance of their family, a gift card to a place that offers family photos could be a great option.

Even a dinner for two to somewhere nice is a splendid gift. For giving gifts, I like to put some thought and feeling into it. I prefer to give something that will last longer than just a meal or a few days. Something that will provide an experience or a memory. For instance, a nice clock that they can hang on the wall or a watch, or a picture frame to display their family photos.

When you're selling a property, it's important to understand that real estate agents rarely provide extra incentives to sellers beyond their commission. Therefore, it's important to establish common ground with the seller in order to build a rapport with them. Spend time on the phone with them, asking questions about their neighborhood and interests. When they mention something that you have in common, acknowledge it and let them know you share their interests. This will help to build a connection with them and make them feel more comfortable with you.

Consider getting them a gift that is tailored to their interests. For example, if they're a fan of a particular sports team, you could get them tickets to a game. This will show that you care about them as a person and not just as a client.

Before the closing date, ask them where they'll be moving to and offer to forward their mail to their new address. This is a great way to show that you're thoughtful, and it can also help to ensure that they receive any important mail that may be sent to their old address. Keep in mind that surprises are always appreciated, so don't reveal the reason for asking about their new address.

Ask the seller for a testimony. If you're going to go see them in person, ask them to make a video if they're open to it. If you do something remotely, then ask them to email you a testimony. This can be a short and sweet testimony with details about how they did and especially discuss what was done right.

A short testimonial on your services from your clients, mentioning how you worked with them, and expressing appreciation for their feedback can be a great way to build your reputation. It's important to give them the gift of great service first, and then ask for the testimonial. When you have their testimonial, it's a good idea to post it on your professional website to build your online presence. You don't need to include their full name, just their first name and initial. If you're operating under your own company name, it's important to consult with a lawyer or an attorney. If you're doing wholesaling in your personal name, then that's easy too. Just represent yourself and ask for feedback on your services.

Chapter 14

Chapter 14 is about Value-Add Strategies. This is about asking the right questions of a real estate lawyer or attorney when you're a wholesaler looking to assign contracts. It's crucial to ensure that the lawyer you're working with has experience in dealing with wholesale transactions and can assist you in preparing letters of intent and offers to purchase. Instead of learning everything on your own, it's best to seek guidance from someone who has already done it before.

Wholesaling is pretty popular. If they haven't done one before, I'm sure you can find someone who has. I believe in the three rules; I believe in reaching out to three different attorneys. Ask the same questions to different people and come to your own conclusions about what's better for you and who you may work with better. It's important to ensure that you're protected when signing a contract and that the other party understands whether you or the title company will close the real estate transactions, depending on which side of the border you're on.

If they mention a specific title company, you can ask for their recommendation. You may also need to ask them to prepare a Letter of Intent (LOI) for you or an Offer to Purchase once you find a property. This is important if you don't have a real estate agent, as you'll need to produce the offer to the seller yourself. You'll need their help with paperwork for the assignment, removal of conditions, and getting that to your investor buyer. Finally, you can ask them to review the offers you submit through a realtor.

Sometimes, you're going to have a real estate agent who's going to write the offer to purchase. You want to find out if a lawyer can look over your offer just to make sure that the realtor did their job. It's advisable to seek professional help to formalize a document and inquire about the turnaround time. A lawyer may not work that fast. I've had to find other lawyers that were actually available to close things quicker and ask if there is an extra fee.

Another important question to ask the attorney is about the location of the property. You should inform them which state, province, and city the property is in and inquire if they need to be present in that location or where you live. This will determine whether you need to sign the documents in person or remotely. You should ask about their experience as a lawyer, how long they have been practicing, which areas they specialize in, and whether they can handle deals in your desired location. This information will help you determine if you need to travel to their location and if they are the right fit for your needs.

Ask them what city they're in. Do they do multiple cities, states, or provinces? Are they on both sides of the border? I have a lawyer who will help us, but I need to know how many investors deals they have closed on both sides of the border. This is important because you may have a residential attorney who only deals with single-family homes and first-time homebuyers. However, investors have different needs and a different mindset. So, we need to be clear on whether your lawyer has experience dealing with investors.

If an investor asks me about my experience, I can let them know, "I understand you're an investor and you're curious about the number of investors deals I have closed. You're wondering if I have experience dealing with investors like you, since wholesaling can differ from selling contracts." Tell them you are new, and you have access to a coach to walk you through it all successfully. "Please let me know how I can assist you further."

Questions to ask a tax accountant would be if you should use a business name or personal name? Tell them your three-to-five-year financial goals. Ask them what write-offs are available to you as a wholesaler. What will you owe in taxes on each deal you wholesale? This is not important now because if you're only used to ever working at a job, most of the time, your employer will take taxes off your check, and then give you the rest. The IRS or CRA usually gets paid first. The beauty of being self-employed as a wholesaler is that you get paid first.

The government, IRS, or CRA, needs to be paid second, for sure. They are going to want their money, so you need to figure out how much in taxes you'll owe based on your current tax bracket when you make wholesale deals. If you receive a check for $5000, $10,000, or $50,000 from a wholesale deal, you must determine how much of that amount you need to set aside for taxes. Do you need to keep 10% or 50% of it? It's essential to find out to avoid any surprises later.

A significant question to ask is how can you defer taxes? There are a lot of different strategies, and they can explain what's best for you on that. How can you reduce the taxes that you pay? So again, they're going to refer you to a tax accountant, and they explain all that to you. They're going to give you different tips and tricks to legally reduce and defer your taxes. How should you organize your receipts to give to them? How often do you give them your receipts? Are you able to write off gas, the Internet, cell phone, and part of your lease on your vehicle? You have to bring a vehicle to the site. Are you able to write off the mileage, the wear and tear, the gas on the vehicle? Are you able to write off a certain percentage of where you live right now because you are using it as an office?

It is good to know what write-offs are available to you. For example, can you write off a computer? How do you organize all those receipts and how often do you give that to them? Are you considering selling a property and looking for negotiation tools? Have you contacted a realtor to list the property?

Here's a scenario you can consider: if the motivated seller says no, the wholesaler says great, do you have the money to complete any necessary repairs to the property? If the answer is no, can you wait for 90 or 120 days to sell the property? If the answer is still no, then we can help. We buy properties with no commissions. Is this suitable for you? If yes, we will buy the property as is, with no additional expenses for you. Is this also suitable for you? If yes, we can close the deal quickly. Is this okay with you too? If everything sounds good, then we are ready to help you get the deal done and get the property under contract.

When you ask whether they have contacted a realtor, it is clear they have the option to do so. You just want to confirm if they have indeed contacted a realtor. If they say yes, please ask if the property is currently listed because that is important. If it is listed, then we are not interested. We want to get them to say *No* three times.

This is what we do. No, no, no. Once they're on the train of No, and they realize that you're the only option. So, they've said no to all these things. Now you're coming in, enforcing the fact that you are their only solution. Now you get into our business model. We are problem solvers; we help you move on with your life. We are a pool of cash buyers buying properties at deep discounts. We close when it's convenient for you; we take the property as is; we fix it up to A-plus condition, and we resell it for a profit. Is this okay with you? Yes, great.

It's about transparency, it's about telling them, this is our intention. We are a pool of buyers buying properties at deep discounts.

Now that you have discussed the price and assignment, you can close the deal at their convenience. You have also confirmed the closing date, which will be their choice. It's important to be upfront about how you make money and let them know that you're not doing this for free. Once you have discussed this, you can ask for permission to proceed and also ask for the property address.

After they say yes, you can move on to discussing the property itself. It's best to cover everything else beforehand. If they're not okay with any other part of your business model, then there's no point in finding out how many bedrooms, how many baths there are or where it's located. When you're talking to a seller about a property, ask them about the property's address, how long they've lived there, and request lots of pictures and videos. The seller will try to sell the house to you by telling you about the number of bedrooms, bathrooms, any basement, or garage. Keep listening to them while they talk about their property.

Keep in mind that they're going to be regurgitating a lot of stuff. I would suggest you take notes and then ask what is their lowest sale price? They might ask for $300,000 for the property. When I negotiate, I ask the seller about their minimum sale price for the property. After they tell me, I ask again, for them to tell me their lowest price. This usually leads to them lowering their price a bit or a lot. I then ask about any necessary repairs that need to be done within the next five years. Sometimes sellers won't disclose the information, but by asking this question, I can infer if any major repairs, such as a roof replacement, will be needed in the future.

"When do you need to sell?" This is an important question to ask because it will help determine the timeline for the transaction. It's also important to find out if the property is vacant or occupied. If someone is currently living in the unit, you'll want to know if they plan to move out. Some potential investor buyers may be interested in keeping the current tenants in place, while others may be looking for vacant property.

We have a preference to vacant on possession but clarify if it will be vacated or not. I suggest you confirm whether it's the owner or a tenant who will vacate the property. If it's the tenant, make sure they know they need to move out before the possession date. It's important to address any potential issues upfront so you know what you're dealing with. If the tenant hasn't provided notice, it's vital that you disclose this to any potential investor buyer.

It's important to keep in mind that you may need to negotiate certain terms, especially if there is a tenant involved. For instance, if the tenant is planning to move out, suggest a hold-back arrangement. Let's say you've negotiated the price down to $290,000. In that case, it may be wise to propose a $30,000 hold-back, which would be kept if the tenant doesn't vacate the property on the closing date. This is important because it can be difficult to evict a tenant, and you'll want to be prepared for any complications that might arise. These tips are more advanced, but they can help you navigate the negotiation process more effectively.

It's important to be aware that if you plan to sell a contract that you have on a property that currently has a tenant, it's best to inform potential investor buyers that you intend to provide vacant possession. You can negotiate with the seller to determine what needs to happen for the tenant to move out. You can ask if a vendor take-back (VTB) is available.

A vendor take-back is also known as seller financing, and all that means is that the seller is going to be the bank instead of the investor buyer having to go borrow the money from somewhere else. The seller will lend them their equity in the property. The seller only owes $190,000 out of $290,000. There's a $100,000 difference. The seller could take $190,000 so they can pay off what they owe on the house and then I will hold seller financing for $100,000. That could be an option. The seller could owe nothing on the property and they could decide to loan you or the investor buyer 100% of that which would be the whole $290,000.

Depending on the seller's preferences, the savings of the property can range from $10,000 and up. This is a brilliant strategy. It's important to determine whether the seller works with a title company or an attorney. You should also inquire about any rental equipment on the property, such as the HVAC system and hot water tank. Ensure that any rental equipment is paid in full on the closing date. It's critical to inform the seller of this. It's essential to verify whether the property has any outstanding mortgage payments or taxes.

One thing you can do is to ask the owner if they are behind on mortgage payments or taxes. They may give you a tax bill that will show an assessment of the property. This number can give you an idea of what the property is worth. For instance, if the owner wants $290,000 for the property, but the tax bill shows an assessment of $200,000, they may be asking for too much money. However, you need to do your due diligence and ask questions like whether there is off-street parking, if there are work orders, or if the property has been condemned. It's important to ask about these things because I recently bought a property that was condemned, and it caused a lot of problems. Despite these issues, it was still a good deal, so I closed on it.

Over the course of two years, we got rid of a property we had and learned a lot about the real estate business. Some deals are more about learning than making money, but other deals can be quite profitable. Do you, or anyone you know, have other properties you want to sell? Sometimes sellers have more than one property, and they may know other people who need to sell properties. When dealing with contractors, it's important to ask if they are licensed and insured, and to see proof of this documentation. These questions have been developed through experience, and it's important to keep adding to your knowledge as you grow in this business. There may be things that seem like common sense, but they can be easily overlooked.

Here are some questions you might want to ask before hiring someone to do a job: Are they licensed and insured? You should ask for proof of these things. Also, don't assume that just because they answer the phone quickly, they can start working right away. They might be booked up for the next several months or weeks, so if you need them urgently, that could be a problem.

It is important to ask them how soon they can start a project and ask what city they work in. When you see targeted ads, it doesn't mean the products are in your vicinity. They're just marketing, possibly through Google's sponsored ads that caught your attention.

When you reach out to a contractor, it's important to ask how many people are on their crew. If they have multiple crews working, it's a sign that they are a busy and experienced company. If it's just one person with a hammer and a screwdriver, you can expect the project to take longer. It's essential to develop a relationship with the contractor, not only to get referrals, but also to pass on their information to potential buyers. You must verify if they have experience in roofs, foundation, plumbing, electrical work, and HVAC (heating and cooling system), which is crucial for any project.

Some of them don't have licenses for plumbing and electrical. Some workers do not possess a fall arrest certificate, which prevents them from accessing higher roofs. For instance, if a property has a two-story building with a two-story roof, these workers do not have the proper certification to climb on the roof and perform the work. Ideally, ask the workers if they possess the required certification before hiring them for the job.

If they tell me that a job will take 10 days and it goes beyond that, I want them to know the penalty that they'll have to pay for each additional day. For example, if it's $100 a day or $500 a day, I need to be aware of potential delays because, as an investor, it's going to cost me money. So I need to know there is a penalty in place, and it's best to have a bonus system as well. If you're past your deadline, there's a penalty, but if you finish the job before the due date, there's a bonus. This way, I'm rewarding you for working hard and completing the job quickly. I prefer to work on a flat fee for the job instead of hourly, and setting up a penalty and bonus system is a fair way to ensure that we're both committed to finishing the job on time.

I recommend you ask how much it would be for the full job and not what it would cost per hour when asking for a quote, for a roof, flooring or painting. When you pay them by the hour, they act like they're just their employees and they have all the time in the world. I love the flat fee approach because now I don't have to babysit as much, they know they're not getting paid until the job is done.

It is important to ensure that any construction work that is being done to the property is done properly and legally. One way to make sure of this is by confirming whether the contractors have obtained the permits for their work. If they take too long to get the permits, it is not your responsibility. However, it is important to keep in mind that if the required permits are not obtained, there could be legal consequences for the homeowner, especially if they are an investor. Therefore, it is important to be aware of this and to ensure that the contractors have obtained the necessary permits before they start the work. Sometimes the owner will pull the permit if the contractor does not. If a permit is needed, someone needs to pull them, and you want to find out if the contractor does that part as well.

Are the people you hire to do the work doing it, or are they subcontracting it out to others? It's important to know if you're hiring a company to perform roofing, foundation, plumbing, electrical, heating, and cooling work. If they subcontract out certain portions of the job, you want to know who they're subcontracting to and how reputable they are. Ultimately, it's not just about the size of the company you're hiring, but the quality of the work being done.

I would suggest that you rely on referrals from people you know personally or within your network to find a contractor. It is better to ask someone who has already used their services or has heard of them positively. Based on my personal experience, I have had both good and bad contractors, so it's crucial to have someone vouch for them. This way, you will have a personal reference and assurance that the contractor is reliable and trustworthy.

The most expensive things to take care of in a property is foundation repair, roof replacement, HVAC system, windows, plumbing, mold remediation, termite damage, electrical work, sewer, siding, facia soffit, support beams, water in the basement, and chimney, especially one that's not being used. It's crucial to hire a qualified contractor for any job. If you hire an unqualified contractor, it could end up costing you a lot more money in the long run.

Close on it yourself. You wonder if you can afford it if we close on it ourselves. Some questions to ask a lender are: Are you a licensed lender, a bank, or a hard money lender? There is a difference. A licensed lender can simply mean a private lender-an individual that is lending money. The bank is a bank, and a hard money lender can be a group of people that have put their money together, or it can be an individual who's lending out money at a higher risk, in their opinion, because they're not basing it on anything besides the property and the property value.

They don't care about your credit; they don't care about your job; they don't care if you have any money. They're just there for an equity position. If you need $200,000 from a hard money lender, they'll probably lend you between $100,000 and $150,000. Asking them if they are with the Better Business Bureau is an excellent question because if they're not, then I wouldn't recommend dealing with them. This gives me a great indication of what kind of lender it is. Ask them which title company or attorney they use because if you're going to get a hard money lender or a licensed lender or a private lender involved, they will also want a lawyer.

Be mindful that you are going to have your lawyer if you're buying the property, the seller is going to have their lawyer and then the lender is also going to have a lawyer and you're going to be paying for that lender's lawyer.

To determine the loan amount that you can borrow, you need to consider the loan-to-value (LTV) ratio, which is the percentage of the property's value that you can borrow. For instance, if you are buying the property for $200,000, a hard money lender might offer you up to 75% LTV, which would work out to $150,000 or closer to 50% which would work out to $100,000, while a bank might give you up to 80% LTV which would work out to $160,000 of that. A licensed lender may decide to offer you between 50% and 75% depending on their lending policies. To calculate the LTV ratio, you need to base it on 100% of the property value, which is $200,000 in this example. Therefore, 75% of the property value is $150,000. That's how you calculate the LTV ratio, which is essential in determining the maximum amount you can borrow.

When buying a property from a wholesaler, it's important to know if the lender will include the wholesale fee in the loan to value. You should ask the lender if they will lend you enough money to cover the wholesale fee, as well as any repair loan funds required for the property. It's important to clarify whether the lender will loan you money for repairs or just for the purchase of the property. It's important to ask about the lender's fees, terms, and how long they're willing to hold the financing for you.

You will want to know the lender's interest rates and if they will allow interest-only payments. Interest-only payments are a lot less than principal interest and making smaller payments in the beginning while you're working towards a fix and flip will be helpful. Ensure that you can refinance the loan, pull out cash in three to nine months, and pay off the debt.

If you are considering refinancing with a lender, there are a few important things you should keep in mind. Firstly, check what their minimum loan amount is, as some lenders will only accept amounts of $50,000, $75,000, $100,000, or $200,000 depending on the property. Secondly, find out which cities the lender operates in, as well as how quickly they can close a deal. This is especially important if a seller needs to sell their property within a short timeframe. It's also worth asking what credit score you need to have. Lastly, ask if the lender allows second mortgages up to 100% loan-to-value behind their loan. This means that if the lender is only willing to lend you $150,000 but you need $200,000, they might accept a vendor take-back for the remaining amount. This way, you can get the loan you need without having to put down any additional cash. While these concepts might seem complex, it's important to ask these questions to ensure you clearly understand what you're getting into.

Some people like to live being a wholesaler, which is great, then some of them don't even know that there's a life after that. If you've done your research and you believe that a property is a good deal, you can use the bonus strategy. This involves closing the deal and then listing it for sale the next day. Alternatively, you can quickly clean up the property to make it presentable, which is called *wholetail*. This means that you buy the property directly from a seller on a Friday and list it on the market on the following Monday. You can also renovate the property to increase its value, which is where *fix and flip* comes into play. After deducting realtor fees and renovation costs, you can still make a profit of $50,000 or more using this strategy.

Keep in mind that hard money lenders are also interested in lending for fix-and-flip properties. For instance, I once placed an offer on a property on a Monday, hoping to wholesale it. However, I couldn't find an investor buyer from my list, and the closing was approaching quickly. After conducting my due diligence, I thought it was a good deal, despite the fact that it was a hoarder house that had been abandoned for two years. So, I closed on it that Friday, with just five days to make something happen. It was a rather swift closing, but we were able to clean up the property in time.

I remember the weekend when I went dirt bike riding with my husband and had a nasty fall, cracking a rib. I knew that the closing date for a deal was on the following Friday, so I showed up on Saturday morning to load up stuff into a dumpster despite my injury. We had to use several big 20-yard bins, at least three or four of them. However, by Monday we were able to list it and we doubled our money without renovating the property. The investor buyer took possession in just 14 days. That deal was quite memorable for me.

All we did was remove garbage from the house. We didn't even paint, so there were no materials needed. We swept the floor; mopped the kitchen and bathroom floors and that was it. We left everything as it was; there was no electricity, gas, or heat source. There wasn't even a furnace in the house. To let you know, there are ways to double your money quickly by pumping them out.

Another bonus strategy is to ask the seller to hold 100% financing. As I alluded previously, you can make payments based on a 7% interest rate for a five-year term. All you have to do is tell the seller to act as the bank and hold all the money that you're going to pay. You will make payments based on 7% interest for five years. At the end of five years, you will pay the full amount to the seller. It doesn't cost you anything to acquire the property.

You can rent it out for a higher price than your expenses and also fix, repair and renovate it as required. This way, you can make a profit while improving the property. It's nice to know that you've got some flexibility there. For example, when a lady was selling a property for $80,000, which would be sold with vacant possession. She owned two properties, and this one had recently been renovated because of a fire; the insurance company had covered the costs. Since she already owned another house, she couldn't afford to hold two mortgages at the same time. I don't want to be a landlord. I want to buy a property, but I don't have any money right now. However, if you're willing to let me in with no down payment, I'm interested. To make this work, I used a rent-to-own strategy with an investor buyer for seven years.

I asked to do this because her mortgage was going to be up in seven years. I agreed with the owner to rent her property for seven years at $80,000. To cover her monthly payments, which included the mortgage, taxes, and insurance, I paid her $750 per month. This made me her tenant, and I was able to sublet the property to someone else under the condition that they would be responsible for any damage or repairs needed during the rental period. At the end of seven years, I agreed to sell the property to the subletter for $139,000.

The property was never listed. There were no real estate fees. It went through a few people that were doing rent to own. In seven years, I had three people in there; it was always rented.

I had no money on the deal, but I was making $145 a month. This is creating more money in my pocket. Each time a rent-to-own tenant went in, they upgraded the property, which was beneficial for me. I gave tenants a penalty if they couldn't close on the deal, which meant that I could keep their deposit. Although I don't recommend taking people's deposits, I did my due diligence and ensured that the tenants were positioned for success. Due to their lack of effort to ensure they could purchase at the end of the term, I kept their deposits.

Here's how it went down: the sale price was $139,000, and my purchase price was $80,000. Realtor commission and property management fees were zero because I was managing the property myself. The owner paid for insurance, and I didn't purchase it. I didn't pay taxes as the seller did that. I didn't have to pay interest because I didn't borrow money. I was paying $750 a month and renting it out for $895. I negotiated any mortgage paid down during the seven years was also mine, which worked out to be $15,000.

I had to put in $1000 for some materials when I had a problem underneath the house, but I didn't have any labor or dumping fees.

When I finally had to sell the property as a wholesaler, I had to pay legal fees in between. When I went to sell my contract on the property for $139,000, I had already paid down my debt. So instead of owing $80,000, I now owed $15,000 less. Including the sale and what I had paid down, I got $154,000 ($139,000 + $15,000). I had been receiving a rental income of $145 a month for seven years, which amounted to another $12,000. This brought my total earnings to around $166,000. My expenses included the initial purchase of the property for $80,000 and an additional $2,000. My profit was approximately $57,000. I would be happy to do deals like this all day long, even twice on Sundays.

I wholesaled a property differently where the property never was in my name. It was a long-term wholesale deal. I came across an interesting opportunity where a seller was in a panic and needed to sell his house within 10 days. He had reached out to a contractor that I was using, who then contacted me. The seller wanted $317,000 for the house, which was beyond my budget. Although I considered wholesale as an option, I realized it was not feasible in this case.

However, I had a JV partner, a joint venture person, that I knew had cash. I called him and this was just before Christmas. I told him I have a deal, and I need $317,000 in 10 days and we can sell this property listed on the open market for approx. $500,000. I told him we could split the deal, but it would be conditional upon him providing all the money for holding costs. I requested that when we sell the property on the closing date, I would receive 50% of the profits. He agreed to these terms.

I gave the risk to my JV partner, so anything over $317k was their responsibility. Even if the property didn't sell for $500k, I wouldn't make a profit unless my partner did. Our strategy was to use their capital to buy the property for $317k, which was vacant upon possession. We discovered a small leak that had to be fixed, which was repaired by a contractor. We listed the property for sale on the same day we purchased it. The next day, our real estate agent visited the property to investigate the property.

We listed the property for sale at $499,000 just before Christmas. We expected some low offers, and although we had one interested buyer who agreed to buy it, he backed out. However, another buyer came forward and bought the property for $465,000. We closed the deal 136 days after possession. During the acquisition process, we showed pictures of the property to our realtor. She also helped clear out the snow as it was snowing heavily at the time of listing. Listing before Christmas was not the best time of the year, but we sold it successfully.

When you need to find $317,000, and networking might be the key. You never know who might loan you money, so it's a good idea to have JV money partners on standby. You can even pay a contractor for leads.

Here's a breakdown of the costs:

- Sale price: $465,000

- Purchase price: $317,000

- Realtor commissions: $18,000

- No need for a property manager because there was no one there

- Insurance cost: around $1,500

- Legal fees to purchase: $3,500

This sale was in Canada and land transfer taxes were applied. Legal fees had to be paid for selling the property, and taxes were also due. We had to spend some money on labor to fix a leak, which cost us $300. We paid the contractor $5,000 for sending us the lead. So, the total expenses incurred were about $350,000. The total profit was about $115 - $117,000. We split that 50/50. My share was about $58,000. The numbers are approximate, but they're close.

This is another example where there's no money involved and all I did was put the property under contract and wholesaled it to this JV.

It's crucial to do your due diligence with deals. Even the ones that may seem good at first glance require research to determine if they're worth pursuing. It's important to know the market, values, and what's going on in the industry to make informed decisions. If you're able to make money without using your own funds, it's a smart move to do so.

Always keep an eye out for good deals and seize them if you're able to. Remember, being informed and careful is key to success in any business venture. The key to success in making deals is to do your due diligence. You need to know your market, your city, and the values of properties. Even if you plan to wholesale a property, it's important to know if it's a good deal worth taking. If you can make money without investing your own money, take advantage of the opportunity. Remember, there are good deals out there, but you need to be smart and informed to make the right decisions.

It's important to understand the risks and do your due diligence before investing in real estate, as there is always a possibility of losing money. Even with proper research and preparation, it's not a guarantee. It's helpful to not rely on your own money and ensure that you have a plan to pay back any borrowed funds. Keep these factors in mind before making any investment decisions.

This course was designed to teach you the ins and outs of the wholesaling strategy, so that you can successfully implement it to generate income.

If you're looking for more training and want to fix and flip, BRRRR, multifamily or short-term rental and would like to work one-on-one with a coach that's been actively investing in real estate for 35 plus years, let's chat.

I really want to thank you for purchasing my book. I hope you enjoyed it as much as I enjoyed creating it for you. I've done my best to pour everything that I know from 35 years of my experience into a short-condensed version. I want to literally shave years off your learning curve and to your success.

Thank you, and *until we meet again.*

You can contact me at www.TheresaBeneteau.com or Coachtheresabeneteau@gmail.com

About the Author

Theresa Beneteau has been a hungry entrepreneur her whole life. She worked hard at every *JOB*, knowing that her real estate investing would pay off one day. She delivered newspapers, drove school buses, was a restaurant owner, security guard, handywoman to the building superintendent, and almost everything in between. She was a mortgage broker and assisted many real estate investors maximize their portfolios to over $150M during her 15-year career. She was/is a remote project manager, landlord, developer, and private money lender. She has access to over 1000 active and passive joint venture partners in Canada and the USA.

Theresa's real estate investments have not only been financially rewarding but have also enriched her personal life. They have allowed her to be present for her son's journey into adulthood, retire her husband, and care for her aging parents. Her most cherished roles are those of a wife, mother, and daughter. Over the past 35 years, she has been involved in well over 100 real estate deals, including wholesale, whole tail, fix and flip, BRRRR, Rent to own, equity partner, and lender. Her passion for real estate is evident in her commitment to guiding others on their own real estate journeys.

In short, Theresa questioned traditional paths, ventured into real estate, and persisted through setbacks. Now, she coaches others who want security, financial freedom, and control over their time with little to no money out of pocket.

Other achievements:

- Director in multiple corporations.
- Life coach/mentor for 30-plus years.
- Public speaker.
- Past regional director with a multi-level marketing company.
- In 35 years, she has mentored, coached and worked with thousands of people in the real estate investing game.

You can contact me at www.TheresaBeneteau.com or Coachtheresabeneteau@gmail.com

Top 10 Questions You Should Ask About Wholesaling

https://app.bitly.com/Bo4pjwghIeQ/http://bit.ly/3yvMOxe